EVERYTHING IS GOING TO BE OKAY!

From the Projects to Harvard to Freedom

DR. CATHERINE HAYES, CPCC

Published by Inspired Living Publishing, LLC.
P.O. Box 1149, Lakeville, MA 02347

ISBN-13: 978-0-692-13165-7

Library of Congress Control Number: 2018946472

www.InspiredLivingPublishing.com
(508) 265-7929

Cover and Layout Design: Brand Therapy, www.YourBrandTherapy.com

Enneagram image, page 33: © 2005 The Enneagram Institute. Used with permission.

Editor: Bryna Haynes, www.TheHeartofWriting.com

Back cover photo of Dr. Hayes: Hesh Hipp, www.heshphoto.com

Printed in the United States.

Dedication

To my mother, *Mary Alice*, for being my
teacher for *forgiveness*.

To my son, *Adam*, for being my
teacher for *unconditional love*.

To my granddaughter, *Camilla*, for being my
teacher for the *miraculous*.

To my sister, *Christine*, for being my teacher for *loyalty*.

And to my dog, *Angus*, for being there
and *guiding me home*.

My Dear friend Deb,
I am so happy to Reconnect with you. You are such a special friend...
I love you to pieces. You make me laugh & I love being with you. Let's see each other more often.
I'm glad you like the book!

Much love,
Catherine

Praise for EVERYTHING IS GOING TO BE OKAY!

"*Everything Is Going to Be Okay!* traces a story of personal growth in Basic Trust—from the naïve simplicity of a child to the deep and spiritual faith that, as Julian of Norwich counseled, all will be well. Building from difficult situations in her own life, Catherine Hayes transforms those events into helpful insights and guidance that the reader can use in developing the 'True Self,' and, in this process, covers three tools that she has found beneficial: A.H. Almaas' Diamond Approach, the Hoffman Process, and, of course, the Enneagram."

– **Brian L. Taylor,** Vice President, The Enneagram Institute

"Catherine Hayes's story, *Everything Is Going to Be Okay!*, is inspirational. She has achieved nationally-acclaimed success against the odds. Her path to leadership training is authentic."

– **Chester W. Douglass, PhD, DMD**, Professor Emeritus, Harvard University

"The beautiful blend of Catherine's story, wisdom, and teachings make this book a delight! I found myself literally experiencing the essence of what she was writing about ... and is that not what a great book should do? Thank you, Catherine, for reawakening us all to the beauty and purpose of life!"

– **Rick Tamlyn,** international Hay House author of *Play Your Bigger Game*

"You'll believe in the power of possibility! Dr. Catherine Hayes's book, *Everything Is Going to Be Okay!*, will remind you that, despite your past or current circumstances, you have the power to transform your life. With great depth and vulnerability, Catherine leads readers on a journey of self-discovery and supports them with coaching strategies, as well as the teachings of the Enneagram, to illuminate the possibilities in their own lives. A must read!"

– **Christy Whitman**, *New York Times* best-selling author of
The Art of Having It All

"For each of us who has traveled a difficult path to adulthood, we need to find that one way that best supports our journey to healing, power, and aliveness. In this wonderful book, Catherine shares even more on her path of discovery, healing, and purpose, leading her to her life's work. A truly enlightening read!"

– **Dorothy Martin-Neville, PhD**, speaker, coach, consultant

"Catherine's sharing of her own personal journey beautifully brings to life the true purpose of the Enneagram as a tool for transformation. *Everything Is Going to Be Okay!* is a rich and engaging guide for inner work and transformation, an invitation for inner exploration with powerful questions for reflection."

– **Lynda Roberts**, IEA Accredited Professional, Former IEA President,
Riso-Hudson Certified Enneagram Teacher

"With a compassionate yet strong voice, Catherine Hayes brings us along on a life journey that surely would have broken the spirit of others. Her openness to growth—especially through her exploration of the Enneagram—serves as a map for anyone dedicated to learning how to live and love."

– **Dr. Kerry Maguire**, The Forsyth Institute

"Catherine Hayes's heartfelt memoir is an inspiring demonstration of the power of faith and hard work to move us beyond circumstance to potentiality, and from entrapment to inner freedom. Catherine lets the reader partake of her journey of awakening in a way that touches the heart and informs the mind. A wonderful book!"

– **Leah Chyten**, author, Diamond Approach teacher

"In *Everything Is Going to Be Okay!*, Catherine Hayes goes deep and wide to uncover her fascinating life and inspiring life story and the lessons she has learned through her paths of worldly success and spiritual growth. This is a must-read for anyone interested in the Enneagram, transformation, and spirituality. A+++!"

– **Shannon Kelly, LICSW, PCC, CPCC**

"Catherine's beautiful story of personal and spiritual transformation reminds us how divine we truly are. It began with trauma, both emotional and physical, but the outcome is pure inspiration. She helps us to "get out of our heads" and live from our hearts as we enjoy the freedom and joy of being our best self."

– **Linda Kroll**, therapist, mediator, attorney, best-selling author

"I highly recommend this book! Through her own powerful, inspirational story, Dr. Catherine Hayes shows us that 'there is opportunity for growth in every circumstance and every challenge.' She takes us on a real journey of healing using the Enneagram and other spiritual practices to discover who we really are. Through sharing her own experience, Dr. Hayes reinforces our need to trust ourselves and our own inner guidance. This book is a must-read for anyone on their inward journey to self-discovery and personal transformation."

– **Dr. Debra L. Reble,** Intuitive Psychologist and international
best-selling author

"A great read for anyone who is numbed out by their daily grind, frustrated, and yearning for more and deeper meaning in their lives. We don't have to wait for an accident to smack us on the head to begin! You just need to open this book and be ready to change the way you think about yourself, your life choices, and what you think is keeping you from living a life you really love."

– **Deborah Beany,** Independent Business Consultant and entrepreneur

"From the very first words of this book, Dr. Hayes had my attention and my interest. I could not put it down, even as tears ran down my face as I read about her life. Her story resonated with me deeply and in many ways aligned with my own spiritual journey. You will find powerful questions for reflecting on your life as well as beautifully written stories of her journey to healing. I have been carrying this mantra with me since reading this book: Everything is going to be okay. This is a book of healing, resilience, a return to the self—but mostly a story of hope. Read it now! You will be glad you did."

– **Minette Riordan, PhD,** best-selling author, speaker, and artist

"*Everything Is Going to Be Okay!* is an inspiring personal story which is matched with a clear instructive about how to find one's own truest nature. Using the wisdom of the Enneagram and her experience as a life coach, Catherine Hayes offers a warm and eminently readable look at spiritual growth and its impact on a life. A must-read!"

– **Rev. Diana Phillips,** Spiritual Guide and counselor

"It is with great joy and love that I recommend Catherine's book. I've had the pleasure of traveling alongside her as a fellow student, and as co-teachers of the Enneagram. She brings the powerful gifts of unconditional compassion, encouragement, and kindness to her students, as well as her humble commitment to walk her talk."

– **Michael Naylor, M.Ed., CCPC, LADC,** Riso-Hudson Authorized Teacher/
Faculty, Director of the Maine Enneagram Center for Transformation

"Catherine Hayes has a wonderful ability to explain complex psychological processes with such clarity that they are available to everyone. She uses her own psychological and spiritual journey as a beacon of hope for others, so that the sorrows and traumas of childhood no longer have to remain a prison, cutting us off from life. Her lived experience of gaining freedom from the past using the wisdom of the Enneagram and the Diamond Approach make her a perfect guide and coach for those who want to fully engage in life."

— **Ann Casey, LICSW,** psychotherapist in private practice

"A heartfelt, wise, and powerful book. Catherine's courageous story of overcoming obstacles and rising above extreme challenges is a true representation of divine intervention and stands as an inspiration to us all. Enormously helpful to people looking to rediscover their true selves, Catherine's affirming message of hope and healing is a must-read, and a gem to be treasured."

— **Dona Rutowicz, LCSW,** expert relationship coach

"Wow! In Catherine's sharing of her powerful and poignant story, I feel like she is taking me along and providing me with wisdom to support me in my own journey. What a great tapestry of memoir and wise guidance, both artful and pragmatic at the same time!"

— **Julie Engel, PhD,** leadership development coach;
faculty, New Ventures West

"Catherine weaves a story around self-discovery to find the person you were again. Her ability to combine personal stories and theory make the journey come alive. The phrase 'I felt like a square peg that had been shoved into a circle' immediately jumped out at me and screamed, 'This is what I am!' Incredibly personal, and relevant to anyone wanting something different for themselves in their life."

— **Michael Wallace,** speaker, coach, consultant, and author on leadership

"Catherine has shone a light on a common occurrence for so many of us; losing our essence and direction in the busyness of life. The gift she presents is that there is another way, and there are other choices that can be made. This book is an inspiration to wake up and reclaim your life."

— **Stephani Roy McCallum,** Chief Storm Rider, Courageous
Leadership Project

"For me, Catherine clearly and compassionately connects the dots between her inner landscape and the outer landscape of a demanding world. She speaks for so many of us as she draws the curtain and invites us into her deep experience. What I find so potent about her work is the unique combination of 'mastery and magical.' Catherine guides us through her personal take on the structures and methods she uses like the Enneagram and the Diamond Approach. Throughout, she allows her body to speak in a language every cell in my body can understand, and her spirit to invite me into the beauty of being alive—even if not everything goes exactly as planned."

– **Karen Poel,** founder of the bodyfirst project

"Dr. Catherine Hayes inspires readers by sharing her wake-up call and heartfelt journey that led her back home to her inner truth. *Everything Is Going to Be Okay!* is a beautiful mix of relatable story and practical strategies to connect deeper to your own wise voice within."

– **Emily Madill, ACC,** coach and author of *Fall In Love with Your Life,*
One Week at a Time

"We all have an inner knowing, a voice that guides us. Many of us have lost the feeling of trust due to adverse childhood experiences. Catherine's story of how she was forced to drop into her body and lean into the trust of that inner voice is so very powerful."

– **Nicole Lewis-Keeber, MSW, LCSW,** speaker, Mindset Coach,
Business Therapist

"Compelling, raw honesty! Dr. Catherine Hayes does not shy away from what it took to awaken and change her life. Taking a deep dive into the wounds of her past, she boldly challenges us. She beckons us to live the life that we are meant to live and not the life that we think will make someone else accept us. *Brava*, Dr. Hayes!"

– **Terrlyn L. Curry Avery, PhD, MDiv**, Pastologist

"Raw, open, vulnerable and transparent, Catherine invites readers to accept themselves, begin from where they are, and trust that everything is going to be okay. Even though this is the story of Catherine's journey—her childhood, her pain, her experiences—it is your story, and my story too. This is not just another book on the Enneagram; it gives us a deeper understanding of how we can use it to understand ourselves and find healing as we accompany Catherine as she weaves in and out through the vulnerable and courageous account of her journey of transformation. She instills inspiration and hope regardless of where we are in life, inviting and inspiring us to find our healing through our experiences using the Enneagram."

– **Sheena Yusuf,** Life and Relationship Coach

"Catherine's vulnerability and wisdom are at the core of this book, making the content digestible and immediately useful. Her situation, and how she was guided to shift her perspective and make changes in her life to honor her true self, is inspirational. What is even more powerful about this book is that Catherine uses her story and subsequent insights and learnings to guide the reader to do the same - look at their life through a new lens - the lens of curiosity, clarity, and a new awareness of their truth. I highly recommend the 'Questions for Reflection' at the end of each section. They reinforced the learning from each chapter, and made it personal—something tangible I can do to gain a clearer understanding of what gets in my way, where opportunities lie to take on new perspectives, and how I can make healthier decisions based on my truth. I can't say enough about this book and the way that Catherine masterfully guides the reader through their own self-reflection and growth. It is a must-read for anyone who is ready for a happier, more fulfilling life!"

– **Tracey Lukes, CPCC, ACC,** leadership coach, speaker, consultant, thought leader

"Dr. Catherine Hayes motivates you to dive deep. Her incredible journey from spending decades as a successful, incessantly-busy 'doer' to taking a step away to truly look within, find peace, and discover her authentic joy and passions is beautifully inspiring. Catherine demonstrates the importance of finding meaning in each moment, especially our most challenging ones, as they can propel us to greater purpose and strength. She shows us how to listen deeply to our authentic inner voice instead of living by the limits of our inner critic. Catherine offers readers tools through the Enneagram and coaching strategies to better understand ourselves and what drives us, and to use this knowledge to grow and create the lives we wish to live."

– **Dr. Colleen Georges,** Positive Psychologist, TEDx speaker, and best-selling author

"Dr. Catherine Hayes's book is more than an intimate account of her life, her challenges growing up, and the trauma she experienced. It points to her strong inner guidance that paved the way for her own healing and opened the door to new learning and teaching. *Everything Is Going to Be Okay!* gives readers hope and ways to access their inner strength and find their own truths and authenticity. Within the book are activities and tools that we can utilize to truly understand the depths of who we are. When we recognize our Divine origins and get in touch with our inner guidance and messages, our lives are more meaningful and in alignment with our true selves. Beautifully written and poignant, her book will rekindle your faith and inner strength."

– **Dr. Jo Anne White,** certified Life, Leadership and Business Coach, producer, radio host, best-selling author, and Energy Master Teacher

"Catherine Hayes illuminates the teachings of the Enneagram with captivating raw emotion and vivid accounts from her childhood into the present. Along the way, she turns our attention to the beautiful spiritual gifts revealed in the lessons. As her pathway unfolds, she gently guides us to explore our own lives within the framework of the Enneagram. *Everything Is Going to Be Okay!* is an intriguing, profound journey to the center of ourselves."

– **Deb Coman**, Content Conversion Strategist, copywriter, and speaker

"*Everything Is Going to Be Okay!* is the very book I wish I'd had when I was beginning my own personal development journey and unsure what to do and where to turn. Dr. Hayes beautifully shares how to gain a deeper understanding of self while learning how to tap into one's inner guidance to create a richer and more meaningful life. This is a must-read for anyone who wants to gain a deeper understanding of who they are in every area of their life!"

– **Jeannie Spiro,** business strategist

"This is a remarkable story told by a remarkable woman. Not only does Catherine takes us through her inner journey to personal freedom and forgiveness, she gives us our own map and guides us every step of the way. Her toolbox is the perfect balance of wisdom, practicality, and forgiveness."

– **Anne Geary,** Founder of Enneagram Approach—Education, Transformation, Leadership, and Recovery; member of Board of the Narrative Enneagram, International Enneagram Association Accredited Professional

"*Everything Is Going to Be Okay!* is an inspiring book for anyone that's ready to give themselves permission to explore who they really are. Catherine's heartfelt words offer encouragement and support to help readers see an opportunity for growth in every challenge, and go back to the feeling of Basic Trust and knowing, that at the end of the day we're always loved and supported, so everything is going to be okay."

– **Patricia Young,** Transformational Life Coach and international best-selling author

"Learning your truth opens up your true essence with courage to lead from the heart and power to change the world. Catherine shares a path to ultimate happiness, with willingness to uncover limiting beliefs, where women are led to their inner peace, a knowing that everything is going to be okay!"

– **Jackie Ruka,** best-selling author, America's Happyologist, and certified Success Coach

"The inspiring story and unique wisdom Catherine shares in this book will lead you to strengthen your inner guidance system and develop a solid belief that everything will always work itself through. A definite read for anyone looking to build more inner strength and optimism."

– **Kristi Ling,** best-selling author of *Operation Happiness*

"Get ready ... From the moment you pick it up, *Everything Is Going to Be Okay!* will make you feel—*really* feel—and it's absolutely beautiful. This book and its contents evoke raw emotion and deep reflection. Within minutes, I was completely enthralled. We have a tendency to work to numb ourselves from ourselves. We create a sense of almost artificial purpose. Catherine's stories, work, and exercises cut through that and get you back in touch with who you are, unapologetically! She took me on a journey to accept that I am perfectly imperfect. I understand my connection to my calling on a deeper level and it only motivates me to press on with even more determination. This book will be a game-changer for you if you let it. Connect from your heart, and the changes will flow. I promise!"

– **Teresa Sande, MA,** Talent Expert, author, Fraud Fighter and Fierce Finder

"Not your ordinary book! Did you ever feel like you just need someone to tell you that it's going to be okay? It's almost midnight and I am having a hard time putting Catherine's book down. Her stories are captivating and the exercises are bringing me to an entirely new level. I can't help wonder: What would the world be like if everyone knew they would be okay no matter what?"

– **Nina Segura,** CEO, best-selling author

"Catherine opens herself up to share how her life has impacted the choices she made. It makes you want to look inside yourself and examine how some life experiences shaped who you were and who you are now."

– **Dr. Frances Kim,** public health consultant

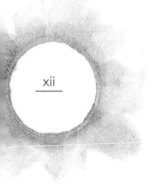

Foreword

Russ Hudson, Co-Founder and President of The Enneagram Institute

Given the pace of modern life, many of us spend most of our time getting by, functioning as best we can, and trying to show up for our people and our responsibilities. We maintain a brave face while internally harboring secret doubts and insecurities. We are not being false—we are simply behaving in familiar ways that we have come to identify as our way of being. But at some point in our lives, we may well start to wonder what life is *really* about. It is not that we have never thought about such things, but we begin to take on this question with more seriousness and focus. This question may also take the form of wondering how to become who we really are, as we sense that there is more to us than we have been showing to others or even to ourselves.

Sometimes, we feel this shift as the need to improve the quality of our lives. We wonder what it would mean to be happier, more confident, more loving, and free from our suffering. If we pursue this question, we quickly discover a plethora of books, teachers, and teachings willing to show us everything from how to organize our closets to how to get enlightened in a week-long course.

This can be daunting and confusing—but if the question is real in us, we will nevertheless dive in and hope for the best.

As we examine the course of our life, we may realize that it is often great challenges and losses that trigger our search for meaning. These profound questions about purpose and identity arise with force after big shake-ups, when our usual coping strategies fail us. At such times, a gap in the usual momentum of our thoughts and actions can appear. While we may be in great pain, we also have a rare glimpse into the deeper needs of our soul. We begin to recognize that, while the ways in which we have been conducting ourselves have their merits, they are not enough to help us through this tougher time. After years of doing our best, we feel no closer to what we truly want. We might even realize that *we are not altogether sure what we want*, and thus, many of our efforts feel futile and empty. The shock of this can be the beginning of a real transformation in our lives.

As this need to change grows in us, we encounter a wide variety of suggestions on what to do, and how to approach this project of change. Do we need to be more spiritual? Do we need psychotherapy—and if so, for how long? Do we need coaching? Or are we fine just as we are? Certainly, our culture provides many incentives to keep business as usual in place, but that question, that longing for something more, can never be entirely extinguished—and, once it is really ignited, we find it impossible to return to the automatic ways of living that got us through up to that point.

As we embark on this new journey, we discover an age-old truth: authentic change is not easy! No one taught us what it entails, or how to go about acquiring the skills that we might need to navigate it. We discover that there are many internal obstacles to surmount, and that our habits—even our bad habits—are connected with survival strategies from our childhood that are not so readily dislodged. We find our habits stubbornly reasserting themselves regardless of how much introspection and "positive thinking" we do, and, if we are lucky, at last come to realize that our personality cannot fix our personality. Our ego does not know how to "fix" itself. In order to grow, we need to tap into something greater.

There are also many external obstacles to growth. The marketplace for "self-help" is vast, and there are many different views on how to approach our development. We encounter books and teachings and methods that promise change—even instant change—but can become discouraged when many of these promises fail to come through for us. How do we know when we have found a real teaching? How can we recognize when we are making genuine progress? And then, when we do begin to achieve real breakthroughs, we may discover that not all of our friends and loved ones are as excited about our new reality as we are. When we begin to change, it creates a need for change in those around us, and so they may experience this as a confrontation with their own inner troubles which they are not ready to engage.

As we persist through these obstacles, we will also learn another valuable truth: that the journey is ongoing, and there is no final answer that will signal an end to our growth. Indeed, we are now embarked on a different way of living, a different way of relating to ourselves and others that will continue to mature and blossom for the rest of our lives. We may become temporary believers in certain perspectives, and feel safer in a new belief system for a while. But strangely, as soon as we get "comfy" in such a worldview, some of the old problems tend to reappear, and we may wonder if we have really learned much of anything. We then get back on the trail with greater curiosity and humility.

So how do we know we are making progress? What are we signing up for in this journey? In my experience, we are learning to live from the deeper truths of being a human being, and that this living from truth *is* what it actually means to be spiritual.

For this, we are going to need lots of psychological insight. We are going to need to learn the history of our own development, its patterns, and the patterns of our family, and we are going to need *to recognize those patterns as they occur in our current lives.* And to be able to do this, we need to cultivate qualities of presence and attention that are really the province of spiritual training—the real meaning of the word *mindfulness.* We learn how to be awake to our habitual emotions and thoughts, and to our behaviors—discovering what we are actually doing and not what we *think* we are doing. We learn to track the various manifestations of our ego—and as we do so, something new begins to grow in us.

What we seldom expect is that by doing all of this we begin to see through our defenses, and that under those defenses are the pains and hurts we have hidden away from our childhood on to the present day. And we discover that to be present and awake enough to observe what is really going on inside of us also *gives us the capacity to hold our distress*. We learn to stop hiding from ourselves and from our suffering so our wounds can finally be addressed and healed. We learn to be more heartful, vulnerable, and human, and this also gives us the ability to show up powerfully with the difficulties others might be experiencing. We discover that this sensitivity actually connects us to others in real ways, and that hiding from our hurts isolates us.

As Catherine Hayes so beautifully lays out in *Everything Is Going to Be Okay!*, the way to the true oneness of reality, to the level of spirit, is the way of Truth: really seeking to be in the truth of our experience moment by moment. This sounds easy at first, but as soon as we actually try to engage this practice, we see that it may take our entire lives to understand even a portion of what this actually means. Truth here is not a simple formula—not words we can memorize. Truth is an ongoing felt contact with our bodies, hearts, and minds that opens us to those deeper dimensions of human experience where real meaning and fulfillment can be found, and this journey will lead us to greater kindness, courage, and humility. As George Gurdjieff, the man who brought the Enneagram symbol to the attention of the modern world, once said, "We are learning to be human beings without quotation marks." We are learning what a human life is really about.

In this wonderful book, Catherine sets a real example for how to engage in this process by sharing the heart of her journey with honesty and vulnerability. She shows us how the crises of her very real life led to discoveries and openings to new possibilities, and how the teachings she learned offered her ways to dive deeper into the core of what was truly occurring in her heart. She helps us see how the challenges and the inevitable hurts in a human life can become the grist for genuine transformation, and that no matter what our difficulties may be, they are workable. They can be transformed.

By sharing some of the tools that she found most helpful on her own journey, and offering reflections for us, the readers, to ponder, Catherine shows us that real transformation is possible for us—we can do it! We do not have to be perfect masters to participate in this great adventure of the human spirit. We can take our own journey with courage and compassion.

Through her story, she helps us see that we are all on this search together, and that there are no "perfect humans" out there who have the whole thing worked out. By revealing our authentic thoughts and feelings and seeing them in a context of grounded compassion, we help each other find the way to a new basis for human relationship and culture. We find that the inner journey is not linear. Rather, it is an ongoing series of challenging encounters with our true feelings, piercing insights, and breakthroughs into new understandings of who we are, what we are, and what this life might be about. And, along the way, we discover others in that journey and create community and mutual support for this process. I personally feel that the future of spiritual endeavors lies in this direction. We are learning to create "beloved community" out of our authentic sharing, our sensitivity to each other and to life, and our receptivity to the deeper truth that lives in all of our hearts. *Everything Is Going to Be Okay!* is an enormous contribution to this process—an invitation to the real and true calling of our souls. I hope you enjoy it as much as I did.

Russ Hudson
New York City
May 5, 2018

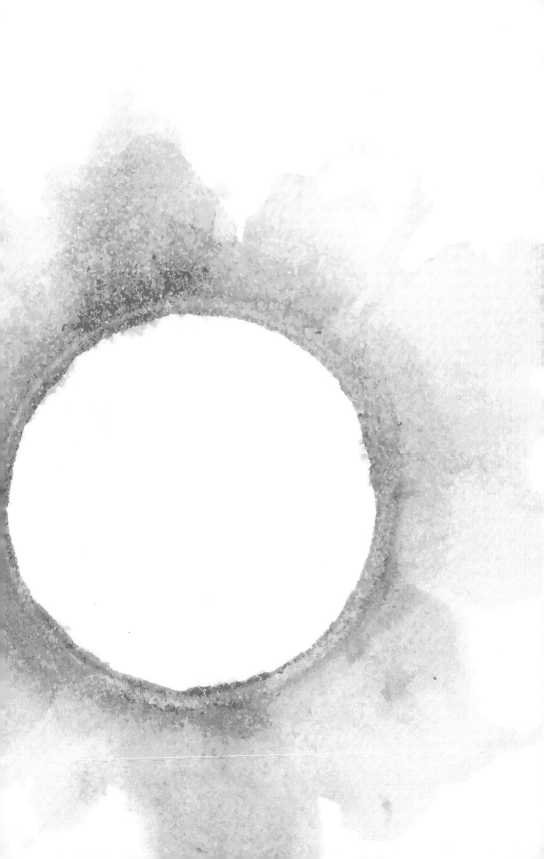

TABLE OF
Contents

EVERYTHING
IS
GOING
TO BE
OKAY!

From the Projects to Harvard to Freedom

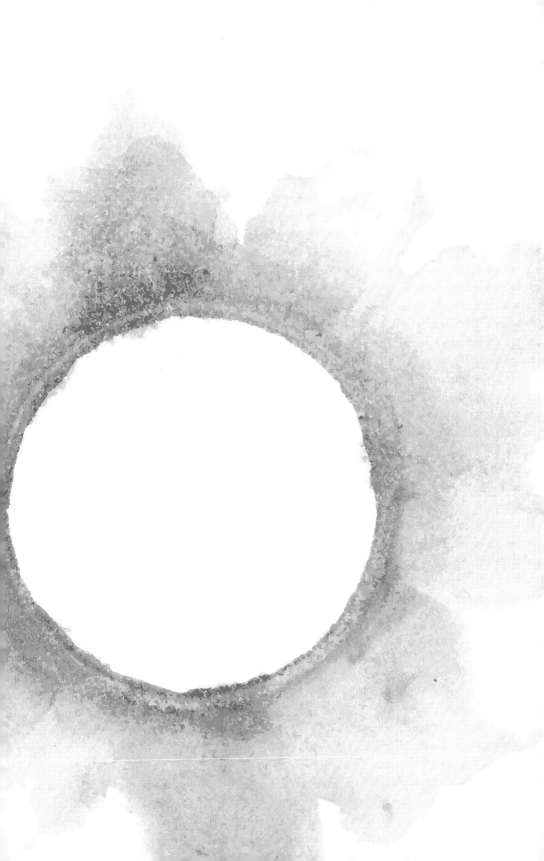

Introduction

On the day I received the message that would ultimately inspire this book, I was six years old, and walking to school through the projects of South Boston. A little Irish lass with red hair and a smattering of freckles, I trudged along with my head bowed and my heart heavy. I don't recall exactly what had happened that day at home, or on the previous day, but since my mother was always wrathful toward me, it could have been anything. I do remember that, as I walked, I wondered what was wrong with me—why, even though I worked hard to be the best little girl I could be, my mother didn't love me, or even like me.

And then, as I paused to look both ways on the corner of Kemp Street and Dorchester Avenue, I felt a sudden knowing, as though a voice had spoken inside of me.

The message was, *"Everything is going to be okay. It's not you, it's them."*

The words felt true, and so comforting. Suddenly, my body relaxed. I felt at peace, as though I had been cradled in the warm, loving arms of Grace. I knew then that it didn't matter what my mother did, or how my siblings acted,

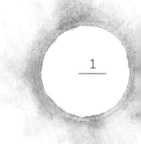

or how much fear I carried. I didn't question the message; I simply accepted it as truth. I trusted that everything was going to be okay.

That message became a touchstone for me throughout my entire life. I remembered it when my life at home was too harsh and painful to bear. I remembered it when I was a single mother with no one to rely on. I remembered it when I was an overworked overachiever with a tenure-track faculty position at Harvard but little sense of my own joy. I remembered it when I woke up from the accident that would prompt my massive internal shift and a journey of forgiveness and self-love.

I know now that what I experienced on that street corner was a gift of Basic Trust—the soul-deep knowing that the Universe is benevolent, and that I am protected, guided, and loved. Until I took a deep dive into my own spiritual journey, I had no idea what a gift this was. Despite my challenging childhood and the huge obstacles I had to overcome as a young adult, I had this message from Grace to trust when times were tough. The words that were given to me at six years old literally saved my life on more than one occasion.

We are all loved and guided in this way, but many of us lose connection with the feeling of Basic Trust. As we go through life, we forget our true, essential nature as divine beings having a human experience. We develop a personality to navigate the world—and that personality is the behavioral manifestation of ego, whose job is to keep us safely within the lines of the status quo.

One of the core messages of this book is about coming back to this supported state of Basic Trust. There is an opportunity for growth in every circumstance, and every challenge. But the more entrenched in ego we become, the further from our true, divine selves we drift. When we take the time to understand the origins and nature of our unique personality, and bring back our trust that everything is going to be okay, we ease the stranglehold of our ego on our behavior. We are able to breathe, respond in a proactive way to whatever life is throwing at us, and embark on our true human journey: the journey back to ourselves.

I'm not famous. I'm not a celebrity. I'm not a billionaire business mogul. I'm a regular person with a very human story that culminates in trust, forgiveness, healing, and a reconnection to my essential self. I was guided on a path of awakening, and it led me to wake up from the trance of living as my false self. My hope is that, through my story and the information I share on these pages, you will see your way to your own awakening and your own reclamation of Basic Trust.

Through my story, I will explore with you the dichotomy of the false self and our true nature, and share some tools (such as the Enneagram, the Diamond Approach, and coaching techniques) for identifying the former in order to free the latter. I have also created journaling prompts at the end of every chapter, so you can explore how aspects of the human story have unfolded within your own experience. When we do this work with compassion and awareness, we can more easily set aside the fears of the ego and the negative aspects of the personality in order to shed our doubts, conditioned behaviors, and self-limiting beliefs in order to embrace who we truly are.

I count myself blessed to be able to share my story with you in this way. My greatest wish is that you, too, are able to step into a state of complete trust and allowing—and that this book will provide you with a path to understanding beyond a shadow of a doubt that, no matter where you are or what is happening in your life, everything is going to be okay.

In love, faith, and joy,

Dr. Catherine Hayes, CPCC

"Owning our story can be hard, but not nearly as difficult as spending our lives running from it. Embracing our vulnerabilities is risky, but not nearly as dangerous as giving up on love and belonging and joy—the experiences that make us the most vulnerable. Only when we are brave enough to explore the darkness will we discover the infinite power of our light."

- Brené Brown

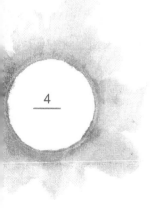

CHAPTER
One
1

THE WAKE-UP CALL

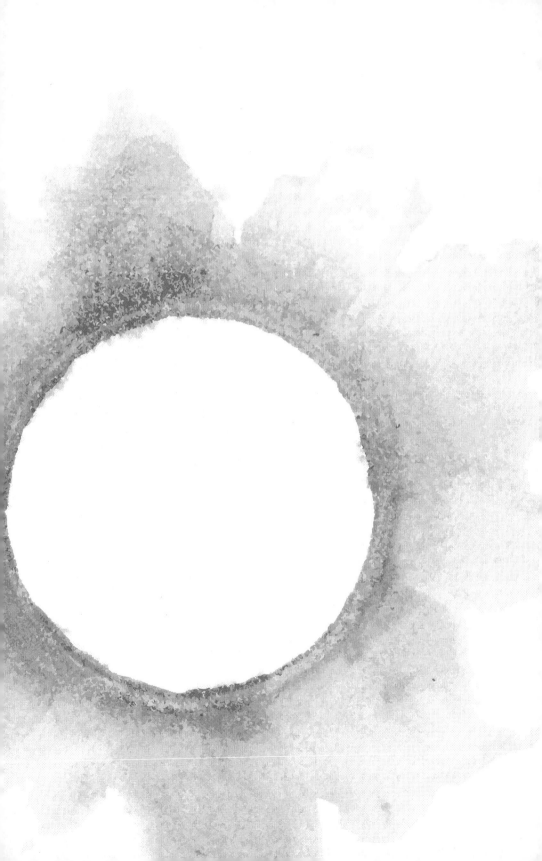

The Wake-Up Call

"*It's time to change your life.*"

The thought passed through me like a thunderbolt as I struggled to regain consciousness. My first reaction was confusion. Where had the thought come from, and why? What was happening to me? Where was I?

Everything was dark. I couldn't feel my fingers or toes, and I wondered if I was paralyzed. I could hear a woman calling to me in the distance: "Are you okay?" Her voice annoyed me. All I wanted to do was to sink back into the peaceful darkness.

A few moments later, the darkness began to lift. A kind-looking older man leaned over me and helped me to sit up. "Are you alright?" he asked. The words wouldn't come. I tried to talk, but nothing came out. What was happening to me?

Finally, I was able to form words. "What happened?" I whispered.

"You fell backward onto the sidewalk," the man replied. "You landed on your head."

I raised a shaking hand to feel the back of my head. The lump was huge. Terrified, I began to cry, which only made my head hurt worse.

In my left hand was a red leash attached to a plaid dog collar.

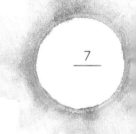

"Do I have a dog?" I asked. "Where is he?"

"Right there, Ma'am." There, to my left, was my dog, Angus, sitting faithfully by my side. I couldn't remember how he'd gotten there, either.

Finally, I felt steady enough to try to stand—but my legs refused to hold me. The man caught me and gently lowered me to the sidewalk again.

"Do you want me to call an ambulance?" he asked.

I shook my head. My mind couldn't encompass the thought.

I sat for a long time, trying to collect myself, and finally tried to stand again. I wobbled, but this time I kept my feet, and somehow I made my way to my car.

Sitting behind the wheel, I started to sob. I had no idea what to do, no idea what had happened to me. Finally, at a loss, I drove the half-mile to my house, and called my neighbor, Randi.

"Hi, Randi," I began. "I feel like I was supposed to call you about something today …" I trailed off as the words ran out.

"Catherine, we just spoke an hour ago. You said you could babysit the girls while Vic and I go to a wake."

I couldn't remember that conversation, and told her so. Immediately, Randi knew something was wrong. "Don't move," she instructed. "I'll be right over." She and Vic were at my door a few moments later.

"What happened?" Randi asked.

"I can't remember anything," I told her. "Maybe I fell on some ice?" I glanced out the front window, but there was no ice, which only deepened my confusion.

I began pacing back and forth across the living room. "I can't remember," I repeated. "It's like my brain is empty.

Nothing is in there. *Nothing*."

Randi and Vic shared a concerned look, and their expressions scared me even more. I was trying so hard to piece together what had happened, and I thought I sensed it had something to do with my dog.

"He looks like he was just groomed," Randi confirmed. "Did something happen outside the groomer's?"

"Maybe," I replied. "No, that wasn't it. I think I remember driving to the pet store. I wanted to get him a treat."

Gradually, Randi and Vic helped me piece together my day. I followed my usual morning routine of tea and breakfast at home. I participated in meetings at my office at Harvard University. I took Angus to the groomer, and then headed for the pet store to get him some of his special bully sticks. I remembered getting out of my car at the pet store while holding Angus's leash and stepping onto the sidewalk as I came around the car to get him out. But try as I might, I couldn't remember anything about the accident itself, or the drive home.

The harder I thought, the more confused and uncertain I felt. Was my brain permanently damaged? Would I lose chunks of my life, and never get them back? I began to cry again; the tears came faster when I felt the enormous lump on the back of my head again. Vic went to the freezer and got me a bag of frozen peas to hold against the contusion.

"I should have let that man call the ambulance," I said.

"I think you're right," Vic said. "Let's get you to the hospital."

Randi drove me to the hospital emergency room while Vic went to the wake they had planned to attend together. In the car, Randi gently quizzed me on various points, like the date

(Thursday, February 3, 2005), the name of our town, and my son's name.

"Don't ask me who the President is," I told her, trying to lighten the mood. "I don't agree with his policies and the last thing I need right now is to get all worked up."

When we arrived at Newton-Wellesley Hospital, I found the triage nurse, and said, "My name is Catherine Hayes. I hit my head and I'm very confused." Her bored look was immediately replaced by concern. She sat me down to take my blood pressure and ask me the standard questions. My blood pressure had climbed to 140/95—way above my normal 100/70—and my anxiety only increased when the nurse ordered a CAT scan. Now, I was starting to worry that there was something seriously wrong with my brain.

After the scan, the doctor came in to discuss my results.

"You have a beautiful brain," she said, which made me laugh.

"There's no sign of bleeding," she continued, "which is wonderful news, but there is some inflammation, and you have a moderate concussion. You can go home—but someone will need to wake you up every two hours."

"I live alone," I told her.

"No problem. Just set an alarm, and make sure it's loud enough to wake you immediately. You'll probably have a bad headache, so take Tylenol if you need it, but no aspirin. Other than that, no driving or strenuous activity for a couple of weeks. Your body and your brain have been through a lot. The best thing you can do right now is rest."

"So ... I can't go to work?"

"Not for at least two weeks. After that, it will be up to your primary care physician."

My mind struggled to encompass this. Two weeks! Other than the occasional vacation, I hadn't taken two weeks away from my work in … I couldn't remember how long. Out loud, I agreed, but inside I was thinking, "I'll be back at work in a week."

Randi drove me home. After profusely expressing my gratitude, I went inside, put ice on my head, and got into bed. I vaguely remember calling my sister, Chris, and my friend, Helen, to tell them what had happened before I fell into an exhausted sleep.

I woke up every two hours, as instructed, and I was grateful every time I did. The next morning, I dragged myself into the living room, and sat quietly in my chair with the newspaper. Try as I might, I couldn't make out the words. Frustrated, I put it down. Apparently, another nap was in order.

Later, I took Angus out for a walk. At the end of my walkway was a small patch of ice. It couldn't have been more than a few inches wide, but the sight of it sent a rush of panic through my body. My neighbor Mike, seeing my distress, came over to ask what was wrong. I told him what had happened.

"Don't worry," he said, calmly. "You're going to be okay. And I'm right here if you need anything."

I thanked him, feeling immensely grateful that I had such wonderful people living around me. Then, I went back inside as fast as I could and shut the door on that slick, terrifying patch.

The next few days were a blur. I called my friends Kerry and Alex to cancel the dinner we'd been planning for months—there was no way I could drive, let alone sit in a noisy restaurant—so Kerry came over with soup instead. I walked my dog, and sat for hours just breathing. I was amazed at how quickly my mind and body settled into this slow, easeful pace. I thought, "This must be what it's like for normal people who don't have to work so hard and run around so much."

Work was the story of my life. I worked as a child. I worked as a teenager, and as a student. I worked as a single mother raising a child with no support from my family. I pushed myself. I studied. I achieved. There was little time for play or joy, let alone sitting still and staring into space. This stillness and lack of stress was completely new to me—and yet, it felt so natural to stop moving for a while, to just *be*.

I realized, over the course of those first still, slow days, how much weight I carried on my shoulders. Everything was up to me. I carried all of the burdens for myself, my child, my career. I was responsible for everything (or, at least, I saw it that way at the time). But now, I wasn't able to handle any responsibilities other than taking care of myself and getting well. Even when I tried to do something, it didn't work. I couldn't read. I couldn't watch television. I couldn't talk on the phone for more than a few minutes. Anything that required my brain to be "on" felt overwhelming. All I could do was be still and heal.

It was as if, somehow, the Universe had given this compulsive overachiever the gift of complete inactivity. My brain and body were telling me to stop, slow down, rest, rest, rest … and in the quiet, a new awareness was emerging. There was a different way to live my life, a different way to be in the world. Maybe things didn't always need to be so *hard*.

I recalled the words I'd heard before I regained full consciousness on the sidewalk: *It's time to change your life*. Right now, a major life change felt like too much for my brain to handle; I couldn't read the newspaper, let alone make any kind of plans, so I let my thoughts wander elsewhere. But deep inside, a process was happening—an unfolding.

In many ways, the accident was a gift—a moment of divine intervention. Looking back, I can see that, although I didn't commit to "changing my life" right away, there were shifts in my thought patterns which took place almost immediately. Somehow, all the minute details of the many things I did on a daily basis felt less significant. My work as a faculty member at Harvard, the paperwork, the phone calls, the meetings and lectures and errands … all of it faded into the background. I honestly couldn't understand how I had sustained that level of busyness.

After the first week, which consisted mostly of naps, baths, and brief walks with the dog, I knew that I wasn't even close to being ready to go back work. After the second week, I felt the same. In the end, I was out of work for nearly a month, and when I did return, I found myself moving at half my previous speed. When I did have to ramp up my schedule again, I found myself resenting it, longing for the quiet, restful silence of my bedroom, or the deep conversations I'd had with visiting friends and well-wishers over tea in the evenings. Things that had once seemed vitally important now held less significance for me. For the first time, I began to entertain the possibility that there was more to life than work and being on the faculty at Harvard. On February 3, 2006—exactly one year to the day after the accident—I went to a workshop with some friends at the Rowe Center in Massachusetts. The workshop was on the Enneagram, and the teacher was Russ Hudson. I had participated in two Enneagram weekend workshops in the early 1990s, and found the system fascinating, but this experience was different. The way that Russ taught the material caused something to stir in me. Something was waking up.

I went back to my office at Harvard that Monday after the workshop feeling like I had been plucked out of a vast, free universe and poured into a tight funnel. It felt weirdly unnatural to be back at my desk, so constricted, unable to move or be creative. The feeling of compression was so intense that I began to cry. And, maybe for the first time since the accident, I consciously realized that I could no longer stay in the life I had created. Something had to give.

My first goal was to learn more about the Enneagram and how it might help me work through the internal shift I was feeling. At the workshop, Russ mentioned the book, *The Wisdom of the Enneagram,* which he and his business and teaching partner, Don Riso, had written together. As I searched Russ's website for the book link, I noticed that he would be leading several training programs in the upcoming year, one of which would take place in Burlingame, California, outside of San Francisco. Wouldn't you know, I just happened to have an open airline ticket to San Francisco (this has never happened to me before or since). The coincidence seemed too great to ignore. At the time, I felt it would be a good personal growth experience. Little did I know that it would radically change my life.

THE MAGIC OF SLOWING DOWN

Before my accident, I hadn't been still in years. Maybe ever. Busyness had always been my comfort zone. I knew I was an overachiever; that was pretty obvious. What I didn't know was why. Honestly, I can't recall having wondered about it at all before the accident. Keeping myself busy meant that I had no time to dwell on the deep hurts and trauma of my childhood; work was the most acceptable way to numb myself. However, coming to stillness after my accident helped me realize that, by keeping myself busy all the time, I wasn't just avoiding uncomfortable feelings, I was also avoiding joyful ones.

When I was forced to slow down, I discovered, perhaps for the first time, the simple pleasures in life. Those walks with Angus, long talks with friends, afternoon naps, and leisurely evenings just being still were nourishing and wonderful. I began to connect more deeply with myself and what I wanted in life. I noticed that what I really wanted—connection, healing, joy— was often at odds with the way I had set up my life. When my calendar was booked solid every single day, I didn't have time for joy. I didn't have time for inner connection. I didn't have time for healing—at least, not until the Universe stepped in.

My accident was the catalyst for my return to stillness. What was at first uncomfortable became delightful. What I used to run from, I began to cherish.

The other piece of learning that came as a result of my accident was how much I relied on my knowledge and intellect as my source of self-worth. In those moments after the accident when I was pacing my living room, I was afraid my brain was empty, and it was one of the most terrifying things I have ever experienced. I'd lived through many traumas, but even when things were falling apart, I'd always been able to rely on my own intelligence and resourcefulness; through them, I could create opportunities, find solutions, and move forward. In those initial hours, when I could access only fragmented memories of my life, I felt as though I had lost my whole self. Upon reflection, I realized how strongly I identified with my intellect and the knowledge I had gathered—and how little I valued those parts of me that were not my thinking mind.

We all have an inner critic—a voice inside us that tells us that we are not enough, that we're not good enough, that we can't pursue our dreams or become the person we know we're capable of being. The inner critic has a comfort zone, and it's narrow enough that it often feels like we're walking a tightrope. What we don't realize when we're letting the inner critic run the show is that, to the left and right of that tightrope, there is a vast universe of "us" to be explored. Sometimes, our true nature and inner wisdom are miles away from our comfort zones; sometimes, they're only a few steps. But until we leave the tightrope, we'll never know.

Comfort zones are funny things, and they look different for everyone. My comfort zone was working hard and racking up accomplishments by living from my head, when in fact, deep down, I longed to slow down and connect from my heart. For some of my clients, comfort zones have looked like inertia, procrastination, fear, worry, doubt, victimhood, or self-sabotage. But while their outward expressions are different, all of these comfort zones have one thing in common: they are

16

designed by our inner critics and built out of limiting beliefs. They are never where our inherent power and strength lives.

We can tell when we are being pushed out of our comfort zone by observing sensations in the body. Most of us are very out of practice when it comes to this type of feeling state—but simply paying attention is often enough to renew the connection and make space for it to deepen.

When we are present in our bodies, we inhabit the present moment; we are not lamenting the past, or worrying about the future. We can become more present through simple exercises like the one to follow, which I often use with my coaching clients. The shift created by this short practice helps to quiet the mind and enliven the body so we can sense the flow of energy.

Give yourself ten to fifteen minutes to complete this exercise.

To become more present, put your feet firmly on the floor and bring your entire focus to your feet. Take deep breaths in through your feet; then, with each subsequent inhale, bring the breath up from the feet and further into the body. Once you have raised the breath through the entire body, sit quietly for a few moments, allowing the new enlivenment to integrate.

Then, focus on your belly center, specifically the spot just below your belly button (often referred to as the Hara, the Lower Dantian, or Kath). This is our body's power center. When you feed your breath into it, you will connect to your inherent strength and inner power, which is always waiting for you.

Next, check in with your body. Notice if there is any area in your body that is holding tension, or that feels "different" from other parts. Focus on that area, and ask it, "What are you holding?" Often this simple question opens up a rich inquiry into something that your inner wisdom wants to bring forth for you to see and pay attention to.

Now, imagine an invisible thread connecting your belly center to your heart center. Focus your breath into the heart center, and allow it to open more with every inhale. Then, ask your heart, "What do you hold for me? What desires, hopes, and dreams?" You will be moved by what is buried in your heart, just waiting to be revealed!

For the final part of the exercise, move to your head center (which by now has quieted down). Connect the thread from your belly to your heart to your head. Notice how your awareness flows freely throughout your whole body. Again, check in with yourself, asking, "What needs to be shared in this moment?" Don't judge what comes up with your mind; instead, let your feeling body tell you if it is true and real for you. With all three energy centers grounded and open, the wisdom that will flow to you is precious beyond words.

The wisdom that comes through when people undertake this exercise is very clear. It's not just about "getting out of your head"; it's about quieting your ego mind so your clear and open mind can be illuminated with true wisdom while being attuned to your body's wisdom. This shuts off the inner critic and allows your true, wise, clear knowing to come on board.

My period of healing stillness was my first major step out of my comfort zone. For a short interlude, I stopped living in my head, and stepped into another way of being. After that, I couldn't go back to the status quo. My next big step came when I said yes to that workshop with Russ Hudson and took my first deep dive into living from my heart.

QUESTIONS FOR REFLECTION

- Have you ever received a "sign" that your life needed to change? What was the sign, and how did you respond to it?

- Where do you think your comfort zone is? What habitual patterns—like perfectionism, doubt, staying busy, or being overly helpful—have you observed in your life? What do you think you are avoiding by staying within your comfort zone?

- What is your relationship with silence? Does it scare you? Does it invite you? Why do you think you feel this way?

CHAPTER Two 2

THE SPIRITUAL
JOURNEY BEGINS

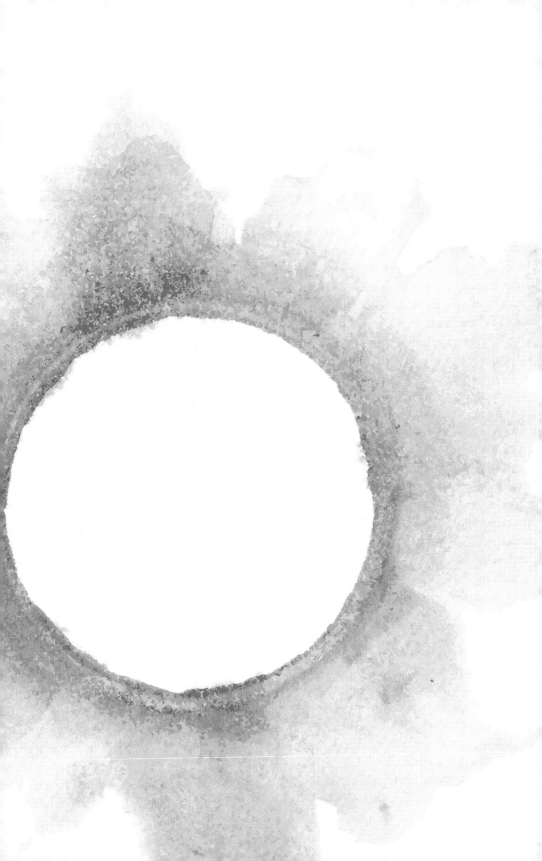

The Spiritual Journey Begins

I had no idea what to expect from the Enneagram Institute Training workshop, but the closer the date came, the more I knew I was on a collision course with something huge in my life. When I arrived at the Mercy Center in Burlingame, California, I felt almost as though I had stepped out of time— as though life had paused to let me take this moment in fully.

The Enneagram is a personality typing system based in ancient wisdom coupled with modern psychology. It has a rich history and the potential to be incredibly revealing and transformative. The name, Enneagram, is derived from the Greek *ennea*, meaning "nine," and *gram*, meaning "chart." It includes nine distinct personality types, arranged around a central symbol, which are related to one another in a dynamic fashion.

I had first learned of the Enneagram in the early 1990s and, based on what I knew, I was fairly sure I was a Type Four, the Individualist. This type is characterized by a sense of longing; of not belonging, and not knowing their true identity. Seeing as I had always had a sense of not belonging in my family and feeling that I was born into the wrong family, this seemed to fit me pretty well, but identifying my type hadn't (yet) brought on any of the revelations

I knew others had experienced. I was looking forward to going deeper—but I had no idea how deep, and how radically transformative, my journey was going to be.

The teachers for the workshop were Russ Hudson, coauthor of the book I'd been researching when I found this workshop, and Gayle Scott. I didn't know anyone else there, which ordinarily would have been uncomfortable, but the members of our group weren't strangers for long. Russ and Gayle created such a safe space for people to open up that we soon began to know each other as deeply as if we'd been friends for years.

As we introduced ourselves to the group one by one, we revealed our hopes and fears for this workshop as well as a little bit about ourselves. Almost everyone said they weren't sure why they had decided to attend the event, but they *knew* they had to be there. There were stories of synchronicities even greater than my own; hearing them, I felt as if the Universe had truly arranged this gathering. I could feel myself opening up even more to both my fellow students and the teaching itself. There was a felt sense of something great to come, something amazing to be revealed.

Russ began explaining the Enneagram and briefly describing each of the nine personality types and the three "centers"—the instinctive (gut/belly) center, the head center, and the heart center—each with a predominant theme and emotion. As he spoke, a new awareness rose within me. I was learning with my whole self, not just my intellect. My body and heart were fully participating in this learning, and I could feel the impact of the teaching in my body. The truth of what he was saying vibrated throughout my being.

Russ explained that, for personality types which operate from the gut or belly center, the instincts are the primary drivers, and the predominant emotion is anger. He went on to say that these three types were not necessarily angry people; rather, anger was simply the predominant emotion that they grappled with. I knew right away that this was not me. Anger was not something I felt very often. It wasn't that I was immune to it, but I was exceptional at avoiding it and burying it.

Russ and Gayle moved on to describe the head center, and how the personality types in this center operate from logic and rational thought, and so often suffer from anxiety or feeling unsupported. Their focus is on knowing and understanding the world, and each type in this center has a particular relationship to their desire for a sense of deep and true knowing and also the fear that they are somehow disconnected from it. Although I was mesmerized by what they were teaching, it wasn't until they spoke of the heart center that I fully realized what this knowledge had to offer me.

Russ began. "The primary emotion of the heart center types is shame. Each type within this center deals with its shame differently, but the Type Three deals with an underlying and unconscious basic fear of being worthless, and so seeks a sense of value from external sources. This often shows up as overachieving. Type Threes, you were probably class presidents, straight-A students, star athletes, just general overachievers. You expend endless effort to be the best at everything, all in an effort to cover up your unconscious fear of being worthless."

Looking around the room with compassionate eyes, he went on. "Often, Type Threes will live their lives for someone else. Most often, it's a nurturing figure: their mother, or the person who raised them. They're attached to this relationship, and to their quest to change its dynamic, so much so that they lead their entire lives for someone else."

A well of grief rose up in me like a volcano. That was me! All my life, I'd tried so hard to succeed, to prove to everyone that I was worthy of being noticed, of being respected. I had worked so hard to achieve success … but for what? Was it because I really wanted that success, or because I wanted to prove to my mother that I had value?

How many times had my mother told me she wished I had never been born? How many times had I tried to make her see—by winning the spelling bees, by getting good grades, by earning multiple advanced degrees—that I was someone she could love and be proud of?

My heart broke. It felt like I was standing on a precipice overlooking a sea of sorrow so wide that I couldn't see the far shore. Everything I had done in my life had been done in reaction to my mother's hatred. I was forty-four years old! How had I not seen this?

I broke down in tears as Russ continued to describe Type Threes' abandonment of their true selves in reaction to their attachment to their nurturing figure. The tears just would not stop; they came from a place deep within. I couldn't stuff this down and forget about it; there was no "managing" this overflow of emotion. In a way, it was a relief to let it all surface.

The sweet young woman next to me, who was from Singapore, handed me a tissue and patted my shoulder. "Are you okay?" she whispered. I couldn't answer. I was falling apart. My emotions were roaring so loudly that I could no longer hear what Russ and Gayle were saying.

Inside, I started to question everything. My success, my degrees, my full-time faculty position at Harvard … were these really what I wanted? If my whole life was in reaction to my mother—and I could clearly see that it was—none of my achievements were really about me. So, who was I, really? How would I ever know myself? Was it even possible to uncover my true self at this point—or was she lost forever?

In that moment, I felt completely broken. And yet, I was aware that awakening was happening. My life, until now, had not been mine—that much was true. But now, I knew what was happening. I knew the truth. I didn't have to live a life co-opted by my mother any more. I could take my life back.

Maybe, I thought suddenly, *that's why I had to hit my head to hear the message that I need to change my life.*

I felt so guided. All of the coincidences that had brought me to this place—including my accident—suddenly made perfect sense. It *was* time to change my life. But I couldn't change a life that wasn't wholly mine.

I spoke with Russ during the break, and told him some of what had come through for me. "I thought I was a Type Four, but I'm really a Type Three," I said.

He nodded kindly. "I think you're right."

Then, words came out of my mouth totally unbidden. "I know that the reason I went through all of this, and the reason I am in the world at this time, is to help people deepen their connection

27

to the Divine." It was as if someone had spoken through me—and yet, I could feel the truth of the words in my heart.

Russ, taken aback, looked at me with wonder.

"You look ... freer."

I felt it, too. A sudden sense of lightness, as though the truth of what I'd just said was a metal cape that I had shed from my shoulders.

Later, those of us attending the workshop were assigned to smaller groups based on our personality type. Since I had previously identified as a Type Four—and, it was later revealed, I do have a Type Four "wing," meaning my personality is influenced by Type Four characteristics—this was my first time connecting with other Type Threes. I sat down with two lovely women, and Russ asked us questions about our lives and habitual emotions and reactions. Then, he played the song, "Hero," by Mariah Carey. The three of us held each other's hands as we listened to the song with tears running down our cheeks. Our journeys, the music seemed to say, were often solitary, but we had to be strong. Most of the rest of the room was crying, too—and yet, I felt a light was shining upon me in a way it never had before.

On the last day of the workshop, I walked the labyrinth at the Mercy Center (which, to this day, is my favorite labyrinth in the world). As I sat down at the end of my walk, I was struck by the sense of solid groundedness and quiet that I embodied. I was so still, so present, without any thoughts weighing me down. It was a state of pure *being*. I loved it. I wanted more of it.

It was difficult to leave the retreat and travel back to Boston.

The airport was so noisy, and people were being so rude to one another. I had just come from a vessel of presence and grace and was now in the midst of egos and hurriedness. I closed my eyes, trying to keep the state of inner peace I'd so enjoyed, and counted the moments until I could board the plane and head for home.

Going back to "real life" after what I'd experienced wasn't easy. I felt that, now that this key piece of my journey had been revealed, I was relating differently to everything—my work, my friends, my family. I felt like a square peg that had been shoved into a circle.

To make sure I didn't lose touch with the ground I'd gained in the training with Russ and Gayle, I signed up for Part II of the training that fall. This time, we met in Kirkridge, Pennsylvania, a beautiful town in the Poconos region. There, I met Don Riso, Russ's teaching and business partner, for the first time. Don was a Type Four with a Type Three wing, and I immediately felt connected to him. When he looked at me, I felt like he saw me, not my job or my degrees. By seeing me clearly, he helped me to see myself, and release the distraction of my ego's desire to constantly do, achieve, and prove itself. I was learning how to integrate my new way of being into my life.

While the Part I workshop at the Mercy Center had been mainly discussion- and information-focused, Part II was more experiential. One of our activities was my first session of holotropic breathwork. I had no idea what it was or what to expect and was a little anxious about it; I wanted to be "good" at it. The instructor talked about how we would manage our breathing in a circular pattern, connecting the inhalations with the exhalations, which along with the music would bring us to an altered state of consciousness where our subconscious mind would reveal what our "inner healer" knew we needed at that point in our journey. Suffice it to say that it was another life-changing experience, and one which was deeply healing.

As everyone in the room breathed together, tremendous grief poured from my heart. My breath turned into deep sobbing, and eventually into angelic singing. This went on for quite some time. I would feel a tickle in my throat; then, pain would radiate from my heart, another wave of grief would wash over me, and I would sob and wail and sing until it passed. When I lay down to sleep that night, my heart actually ached.

We also did an exercise called "welcome to the world," in which one person would lay down in the middle of the group and receive the messages that we all wanted to hear at the time of our birth, such as, *"Welcome to the world. You are so beautiful. We're so glad you're here."* It was profound and deeply moving to both deliver and receive these beautiful, heartfelt messages—messages which, for most of us, were not delivered when we came into the world. In 2013, when my granddaughter was born, I remembered this session, and whispered those very messages to her in the moments after she came into the world.

I continued my training with the Enneagram Institute for several years and became certified in their teaching in 2009. I have a deep respect for this teaching, and for the amazing insights it has brought to me, my clients, and others around the world. I am profoundly thankful for my teachers; I maintain a close relationship with Russ to this day. Sadly, Don passed away in 2012, and although I miss him terribly, I know he is alive in my heart, and that he left an indelible mark on my soul.

RECOVERING YOUR HEART

When my true Enneagram type was revealed to me, it helped me to see with greater clarity and compassion the unconscious patterns of my ego. For me, those patterns looked like constant striving and busyness. I had abandoned my own heart's desire to prove to someone else that I had value.

How many of us have abandoned our hearts in both overt and subtle ways? How many of us wait for the outside world to recognize us before we can own our value? How many of us make choices just so we can fit in, or please someone else, or be seen in a certain light by society? We don't always do this consciously. We get distracted or sidetracked. We feel cornered, overwhelmed, or incapable. And, at some point, we stop listening to that internal wisdom, and start living for someone, or something, other than ourselves.

Although this might sound dramatic, it's all too common. As we become conditioned to live from our ego-selves, and as we receive positive (or negative) reinforcement from the world around us, we move further and further from the truth of who we really are.

Learning about who we are—about the *real* us, not the people we want to be or have conditioned ourselves to be—is one way to begin the recovery of our hearts. When something in our lives (like the Enneagram) flips that light switch inside us, we wake up out of the subconscious patterns we've been living in and start looking for the truth.

If you have an inner kernel of knowing that you have pulled away from your truth, there is no need to judge yourself. This is all part of our human journey. "Waking up" is a gift that so many people never receive; it gives us a second chance at life, a way to reframe and heal all of the wounds we thought would never close.

The first stage of waking up is opening your heart and mind to who you truly are. When you do that, you can stop trying to "fix" yourself, and simply accept who you are without needing to fit in. For me, learning about my Enneagram type opened up a whole new realm of acceptance and clarity around the "real" me. Not only was I not an anomaly, my struggles were part of my divine patterning. Once all of me was revealed, I was able to clearly see a path out of the suffering I had been locked in for so long. More, I was no longer alone; there were others out there who shared my struggles, and who thought and felt as I did.

Below, I will share some basic information on the nine Enneagram personality types. Chances are, you will gravitate to one or two of these types strongly. (If you're not sure what your type is, you can take the RHETI Enneagram assessment test at www.Tests.EnneagramInstitute.com.)

The Enneagram Chart

Courtesy of The Enneagram Institute
Copyright 2005, The Enneagram Institute. All Rights Reserved. Used with Permission.

As you can see, the nine personality types are arranged around a symbol, which shows the interactions among the types. Each type not only has its own characteristics, but also brings on aspects of other types depending on what is going on for the individual. When we are under stress, we take on aspects of our point of stress; conversely, when things are going well for us, we take on aspects of our point of integration. For example (as you can see if you follow the arrows), a Type Five personality might take on the negative aspects of the Type Seven when stressed, and move toward the higher aspects of the Type Eight (its point of integration) when centered and feeling empowered.

I share this not to confuse you, but to help you identify your type more clearly. As you read the descriptions below, think of your "baseline" personality, the way in which you interact with yourself, others, and the world on a day-to-day basis, and how this has played out over your lifetime. This will help you discern which type truly represents you, and which may only represent you when you are feeling stressed or obstructed.

As you read, pay attention not only to your thoughts, but to the sensations in your heart and body. What does your intuition tell you about your type?

Type One: When the personality is in control, there is a need for order, and for everything to be perfect. People with this predominant personality type often become taskmasters. Freedom from their personality comes through letting go of the need for everything to be perfect and accepting that their own true inner guidance is their best authority relieving them from reliance on their inner critic.

Type Two: When the personality is in control, there is a need to be seen as helpful, kind and nurturing. This often comes at the expense of their own self-care, which breeds resentment. Freedom from their personality patterns comes from trusting that they are lovable and worthy and that they do not have to constantly prove it by their self-sacrificing behavior toward others.

Type Three: When the personality is in control, there is a need for achievement and success and to be seen as successful. Freedom from their personality patterns comes from connecting with their hearts deeply and accepting that their value comes from who they are and not what they do.

Type Four: When the personality is in control, there is a need to stand out and be unique to cover up for the lack of a sense of identity. Freedom from their personality patterns comes when they let go of their story and the belief that they are somehow flawed. At their best, Type Fours accept themselves and appreciate their strengths of appreciation of beauty, creativity, and intuition.

Type Five: When the personality is in control, there is anxiety that comes from a sense of not being capable and therefore these individuals tend to withdraw into their own mind. Freedom from their personality patterns comes when they feel confident in connecting to the world and their heart.

Type Six: When the personality is in control, there is anxiety around the sense of having no support or guidance. Freedom from their personality patterns comes from letting go of the need to look to others for answers and trusting their own inner authority.

Type Seven: When the personality is in control, there is an endless search for joy and freedom and aversion to pain. Freedom from their personality patterns comes from appreciating their experiences and no longer looking for excitement and fulfillment in endlessly pursuing new opportunities. They become satisfied with their life and feel a sense of contentment and appreciation for life.

Type Eight: When the personality is in control, there is a need to control people and situations, and not to allow vulnerability. Freedom from their personality patterns comes from letting go of the need to be in control becoming more openhearted and vulnerable, allowing the gift of true strength to emerge.

Type Nine: When the personality is in control there is a need to stay connected to others; therefore peace and harmony become the motivation. Freedom from their personality patterns comes when Type Nines can embrace reality with presence, accepting all of their emotions and becoming truly present and self-accepting.

Each of these types is also correlated with a particular "center"—the instinct/gut/belly, the head, or the heart. As I mentioned earlier, a type's primary center determines its underlying emotions and reactions.

In the instinctive or "gut" center, the three types (Eight, Nine, and One) are predominantly focused on creating a sense of autonomy and respect. This shows up differently for each type. For example, for the Type Eight, the *Challenger*, it's important to feel a sense of control. However, if Type Eights allow themselves to be more vulnerable and open their hearts, this brings on the highest aspect of the Type Two, their point of integration, and they can lead from a place of strength and heart. Rather than having to prove their strength, their inherent strength shines through for all to see.

Type Nines, The *Peacemakers*, tend to be very accommodating while suppressing their own wants and desires. As they become more grounded in their own desires, they bring on the highest aspect of Type Three, their point of integration: courage, authenticity, and inspiration. They begin to speak their wants and desires and pursue them without fear of losing the connection to others or to the world.

Type Ones, The *Perfectionists*, are principled, rational and disciplined, and create a life in which they're seen as perfect. However, as they become more aware of these patterns and more present to their reactions, they bring on the higher aspects of Type Seven, the *Enthusiast,* and cultivate an appreciation for joy and freedom.

The Enneagram types of the head center (also called the thinking center), are motivated to seek support and guidance. The unconscious belief that they are not supported leads to anxiety and fear.

For the Type Five, The *Investigator*, there is a sense of being incapable in the world. As a result, this type holds back from fully engaging in the world and in relationships. As they become more aware of this fear and gain more confidence from developing their expertise in certain areas, they are able to step into the world more fully, bring on higher aspects of the Type Eight (their point of integration), and become confident leaders.

For the Type Six, The *Loyalist,* anxiety results from not feeling supported or guided. As a result, the personality tries to create support by having everything figured out and planning for every worst-case scenario. As Type Sixes learn to trust themselves, and are therefore able to trust they are guided and supported from within, they become less fearful. They can then bring on the higher aspects of the Type Nine, their point of integration, and become more grounded in their true state of being.

Type Sevens, The *Enthusiasts*, craft a life around freedom from pain and suffering. Although they may look like they are the life of the party to others, they're actually dealing with the anxiety of not wanting to live with discomfort. As they become less attached to their personality, they move towards the higher aspects of Type Five, which brings clarity and quiet to their minds.

For the Enneagram types of the heart center, shame is the primary emotion, and the predominant theme is "How do I want to be seen?" For the Type Twos, the *Helpers,* the personality is developed in response to the unconscious belief that they are unloved and unlovable, thus their need for validation and love from others. As they find love within themselves, they bring on the healthy aspects of Type Four: creativity, sensitivity, compassion, and self-expression.

Type Threes, the *Achievers,* feel that they need to prove their value through their achievements. They seek validation from external sources, and have a strong need to be seen as successful. When they connect to their true sense of inherent value, they bring on the healthy aspects of Type Six, their point of integration, and become committed to their communities, where they no longer need to be the shining star.

For Type Fours, the *Individualists,* the unconscious fear is that they have no identity, and therefore they need to stand out as special and unique by creating a false identity. They have a tendency toward brooding and dwelling in their emotions. When they are at their best and are self-accepting, they bring on the higher aspects of Type One, their point of integration, and become more engaged in reality, often finding a social cause to participate in.

***

Our personality, in relation to the Enneagram, is our ego (which is separate from our superego, aka our inner critic). Our ego/personality is the part of us which is human, but it is not the totality of who we are. We are all divine beings having a human experience; the Enneagram recognizes both our wholeness and our human feelings of separateness.

It is believed that we are born with our Enneagram type, and that our type, combined with our life experiences (especially early life experiences in childhood and adolescence) together create our unconscious and subconscious behavior patterns and belief systems. As we become aware of our Enneagram type and how it influences the way we operate in the world, we can begin to wake up to those unconscious patterns, and either release them or learn not to be driven by them. As we become more conscious of our feelings, thought patterns, and behaviors, we can live more from our essential, true self, the part of us that embodies all the gifts of our divine nature.

When I work with clients one on one, teach workshops, or coach in organizations, I guide people to determine their

Enneagram type and to look at what they need to let go of to be free from the ego/personality. However, truly examining our personality requires both intense self-reflection and deep self-compassion. All of us have blind spots around our behaviors. We also have a multitude of tools we can use to lift those veils, such as meditations, journaling, and working with a trusted partner like a coach or therapist. It's all about what works for you, and helps you feel supported.

It's also important to know that it can be challenging for people to accept their Enneagram type for a variety of reasons—most notably that the ego doesn't like to be called out. The ego wants to hold onto its job of defining us as individuals, when in fact we are so much more than our egos. Once we understand our primary Enneagram type and are able to be present to our behavior patterns and reactions, we are more able to accept and appreciate the many gifts of our type and find our path of growth. Compassion is always at the center of this exploration.

So, if you're holding any judgment about your Enneagram type or the aspects of your personality you've uncovered thus far, please let them go. The truth is, we're all perfectly imperfect. Our human journey involves accepting this imperfection without judgment and doing our best to overcome our own personality challenges, especially those that are harmful to others. This is our most important path of growth.

Since waking up to my identity as a Type Three, I have begun to unravel the many patterns of behavior that kept me trapped in busyness and unconscious doing for so many years. In order to do this, I had to go back and actually look at the memories of my childhood I had kept locked away for so long. I needed to understand how my life was built around this unconscious belief that I was not worthy, and that I needed to constantly strive to please. I needed to find and process the moments when I had abandoned my heart, so that I could fully recover it and live as a whole, integrated human being.

QUESTIONS FOR REFLECTION

- Based on what you've read so far, what do you think your Enneagram type is, and why?

- What about this personality type resonated with you? What did you learn about yourself?

- What habits, behaviors, and thought patterns do you now recognize as belonging to your Enneagram type? Do you feel those patterns serve you? If not, what support do you need to change them?

CHAPTER Three

BACK TO THE BEGINNING

Back to the Beginning

As I shared in the introduction, I received a message while walking to school when I was six years old. The first part of the message was, "Everything is going to be okay."

The second part of the message was, "It's not you. It's them."

The first part of the message was divine. It felt like love had wrapped me up in its arms. The second part of the message felt like vindication. As the scapegoat of my family, most days were difficult, to say the least, and everything was certainly *not* okay.

My father was a good man. He went to church every day, right up until he was too ill to walk and was bedridden in the hospital. When I was young he also suffered from powerful delusions, and was diagnosed with paranoid schizophrenia.

Dad was terrified of a Russian invasion (these were the days of the Cold War, so Russia was on everyone's mind), and on one occasion herded us all into the basement of our home in South Boston to hide from the "Commies." He had a rifle in his hands, and my brothers and sisters, all older than me, were scared and crying. I think I was about five or six years old. I tiptoed over to the window to look for the invaders and, seeing that the street was

empty, went to my father and told him that we were going to be okay, that there was no one coming. I wasn't afraid; living with my family, I'd had to become numb to fear, and in situations like this when everyone else was panicking, someone had to be in control.

Not long after that incident, my dad was hospitalized. I didn't know he had been taken away until I woke up one morning and he wasn't there. Some weeks later, my neighbors, Mike and Peggy, took me and my sister Christine to the hospital to visit him, but they wouldn't let us in because we were too young. Instead, we waited outside until he came to the window of his room and waved to us. He looked so sad and thin that it broke my heart. That image of my dad in the window is indelibly etched in my consciousness to this day.

My father was a loving man. He always told me that he believed in me, and I knew that, despite his limitations, he loved me. My mother, on the other hand, wanted nothing to do with me, and made sure I knew it every day.

My first memory of knowing something was amiss is from when I was about three years old. My mother often told me that she had taken the wrong baby home from the hospital—that I was a castoff from some rich family in Newton or Wellesley, or another of Boston's affluent suburbs, and that I didn't belong with her and my siblings in rough-and-tumble South Boston, where nine of us lived elbow-to-elbow in a two-bedroom apartment in the public housing projects. Of course, as a three-year-old, I had no idea what "Newton" or "Wellesley" meant; all I knew was that I was different, and somehow that made me unacceptable.

My siblings, mimicking my mother, often regurgitated her

taunts. One day, my brothers and dad were painting one of the upstairs bedrooms in a mint green color. I really wanted to help, but they kept telling me, "You're too young."

"I'm old enough," I declared. "I want to help."

"Go away," my brother sneered. "You're adopted anyway. Go back to where you belong."

I headed downstairs to the kitchen, where my mother was working on lunch.

"What's 'adopted?'" I asked.

She didn't answer, only dropped the bread she was slicing and marched upstairs. I could hear her yelling at my brother. "Stop telling her that. She'll get *ideas*." Then, they all laughed.

Throughout my whole childhood, I knew that my mother hated me. This wasn't a child's construction. She *told* me that she hated me, and that she wished I had never been born. She told me she wished I wasn't her daughter, and that someone would come and take me away. My father always defended me, but he was battling his own demons, and I don't think he had the strength to stand up to the woman he called "O.B."—short for O'Brien, her maiden name. Every time he spoke up, she shot him down, too.

I understand now that my mother was seriously ill, and that her illness was what spoke to me with so much hatred. But as a child, I could only internalize that her behavior was a reaction to me, since she wasn't this cruel to anyone else in the family. I was certain I had done something wrong—something *awful*— to merit this kind of ridicule, but how could a three-year-old have done something so wrong as to deserve such treatment? Why was I the target of all of her hate, instead of my sisters and brothers? I couldn't find an answer, so I set my mind to being as "good" as I could be. *Maybe,* I thought, *if I'm just good enough, she will want to be my mother.*

Often, I would go to church by myself on Sundays, and pray to God to make me the best person I could be. It was important to me to be a good person, because my mother always made me feel like I was bad. I don't remember ever feeling like I could run or play freely; I always had to be doing something "better," something productive and pleasing. As ill-defined as my mother's lines were, I tried my best to stay within them.

In first grade, I won all of the spelling bees at Saint Mary's school. I vividly recall standing on the side of the classroom in my green plaid uniform, white blouse, and the green bow tie which I thought looked nice with my red, curly hair. I was so proud of myself as I remained standing and spelled all of the words correctly, and one after another of my classmates sat down. *I'm good at something!* I thought.

For each spelling bee I won, I received a stuffed animal. At the end of the day, I had a whole box full of them. I was so elated that I skipped home from school along Kemp Street, and right up to our door on O'Callaghan Way. When I showed my mom the box of stuffed animals and told her how I'd won all the spelling bees, her face darkened with rage.

"You don't deserve those," she hissed. "Give them to your brother."

I remember crying as I handed over all of my prizes—including my favorite, a stuffed bunny—to my little brother, who was still in his crib.

I never heard the words, "Good job," from my mother. I

never heard, "I'm so proud of you." She was just angry with me all the time. She was angry at me for being born. She was angry with me for being born on *her birthday*, of all days. When I did something good, she made it feel bad. And when I did something "bad"—like losing the ruby ring my grandmother had given me for my first communion—she made it feel even worse. No matter what I did, it seemed to reinforce her belief that I was wrong, a disappointment.

And yet, I don't ever recall feeling truly angry at her. I felt confusion, and shame, and I questioned why I should be singled out as the family scapegoat, but I never felt the kind of raw, hot anger that others in my position might have. I knew, even as a child, that my mother was sick, just as my father was. I recall visiting her in the psychiatric hospital after she'd been there for a few days. She'd had a nervous breakdown and had just undergone electric shock treatment. She looked so weak and sad. That day, she gave me one of the only gifts I recall receiving from her as a child: a little coin purse that she'd made for me and my sister. I held onto that purse for many years. It was a reminder that I had to be strong and not fearful. I could not be angry at my parents, who were both so impaired. I had to bury my feelings, and keep being as good as I could be.

And yet, I *was* angry. Of course I was. I had just learned to bury it at such an early age that I had no memory of being angry; it had all been transmuted into shame by my natural tendency as a Type Three personality. I didn't want to hate my mother; I wanted to love her, and make her happy. And so I created the cycle of overachieving that was revealed to me in that first transformative Enneagram workshop.

UNRAVELING THE THREADS

Sometimes, we have to look back to be able to move forward.

For me, the first step toward healing was the realization that I needed to heal—that I had been living my life on an unconscious tether, never able to move out of my mother's sphere of influence. I was in pain, I just didn't know it. I was asleep to my pain. I had become so accustomed to being shunned and abused that I developed the self-protective mechanism of not feeling anything at all. All of my hard work and accomplishments were meant, in the end, to numb the pain—to keep it asleep.

The second step toward healing was actually *feeling* the emotions I had ignored for so long.

One of my first sensory memories after my life-changing accident was a profound sense of numbness which radiated to the tip of every finger and toe. I thought I was paralyzed. As the feeling came back, I was able to move again; later, reflecting on this, I experienced a wave of gratitude for the simple ability to wiggle my fingers and toes. Getting in touch with my numbed emotions was similar. I had been so numb for so long that I was emotionally paralyzed. That numbness kept me locked into my unhealthy Type Three pattern of living for my mother and not for myself.

Shaking off my emotional numbness was painful, in the same way that it's painful when blood comes rushing back into your leg after you've been sitting on it too long, or when your fingers start to thaw after a long time outside in the cold. It hurt to feel all of these emotions, but I also knew it was part of a greater process and that there was healing in sight. The pain was there not to increase my suffering, but to set me free to find the truth of who I was.

Although all of us have our own unique experiences and personality types, we can all benefit from looking back at our early years and unraveling the patterns created there which no longer serve us. When I work with clients, we use the Enneagram, as well as breathwork and other tools, to access these layers without judgment. Our childhood patterns become ingrained deep in our consciousness, and can put us on a path that competes with our inner knowing. Undoing our childhood patterns requires self-knowledge, self-compassion, forgiveness, and connecting to a deeper truth. This spiritual work is just that—work—but it's the most important thing we can do if we want to live authentically and peacefully, from the truth of who we really are. When we release these patterns of numbness, suffering, or avoidance, we can reconnect to our inner knowing and finally move forward.

In addition to our early life conditioning, each Enneagram type has a particular way in which their personality is trying to compensate for the perception that it has lost something from its true, divine nature. For me, the loss of my sense of inherent value drove me to overachieve and become a "pleaser." For others, the loss could be the essential qualities and inherent gifts of aliveness, unity, sacredness, freedom, identity, clarity, inner guidance, or love.

If we are to be free from our personality's patterning, we need to identify what our subconscious mind feels we are "missing." Most of the time, this emptiness or loss is supported

51

and reinforced by our life experiences in some way. When we let go of our conditioning, we also make room for the deep wound of separation to heal. This is the path to freedom, and it is unique for each Enneagram type.

> *Type One:* The essential quality that the personality is trying to mimic is a sense of goodness or sacredness. This leads to an unconscious need to be seen as "good," and to behavior consistent with perfectionism. Deep down, Type Ones fear being cut off from goodness, and that there is something fundamentally "wrong" with them. Freedom from their personality comes from seeing their inherent goodness and accepting that their inner guidance and intuition can replace their inner critic as their best and highest authority.

> *Type Two:* The essential qualities that the personality is trying to mimic are love and sweetness. When the personality is in control, there is an endless need to be seen as helpful and kind, even to the point of self-sacrifice and exhaustion. This results in anger, and can lead the Type Two to manipulate people and situations so they are seen as helpful and indispensable. Once they truly see and accept their inherent loving nature, they no longer need to prove it externally by sacrificing themselves for others.

> *Type Three:* The essential quality that the personality is trying to mimic is value. This results in behavior consistent with a self-image of being outstanding and successful— recreating a sense of value from the outside world. Freedom from their personality patterns comes from connecting with their emotions, from which they were previously cut off.

Value no longer comes from external sources, but rather from an appreciation for their own inherent value, a quality of their being.

Type Four: The essential quality that the personality is trying to mimic is a sense of identity. When the personality is in control, there is a need to be seen as special and unique. Freedom from their personality patterns comes when Type Fours let go of the belief that there is something "wrong" with them, and accept themselves fully.

Type Five: The essential qualities that the personality is trying to mimic are clarity and illumination. When the personality is in control, there is anxiety that comes from a sense of being incapable leading them to withdraw into their own minds, where they attempt to solve problems before sharing their solutions with others. They often become experts in a particular area, and find their connection to the world through bringing their gift of clarity to their work. Freedom from their personality patterns comes when they feel confident in connecting to the world authentically, from their hearts, instead of always needing to have everything figured out.

Type Six: The essential quality that the personality is trying to mimic is guidance. When the personality is in control, there is anxiety around the sense of having no ground beneath them; this leads to the need to have things figured out to the Nth degree. At their best, Type Sixes are grounded, and trust their inner guidance because they know that they are fully supported by a benevolent universe.

Type Seven: The essential qualities that the personality is trying to mimic are joy and freedom. When the personality is in control, there is an insatiable appetite for new and exciting experiences, and intolerance for any sense of constriction. At their best, Type Sevens deeply appreciate the gift of life and all of their experiences, so they no longer have to look for excitement and fulfillment through the endless pursuit of new opportunities.

Type Eight: The essential qualities that the personality is trying to mimic are realness or aliveness. When the personality is in control, they have a strong need to be in control, which can result in behavior that is intimidating and confrontational. When they connect with their heart, they can be truly vulnerable and find the strength within.

Type Nine: The essential quality that the personality is trying to mimic is unity or oneness. The personality can never recreate this fully; this leads to accommodating behavior, and to "keeping the peace" at all costs. Freedom from their personality comes when they fully inhabit their own sense of self, thus embodying a grounded state of being which is inherently connected to all.

No matter what your type is, look at how the patterns described above have shown up in your life. Is there a particular moment from your past that exemplifies this pattern? As you compassionately examine your patterns, pay attention to your feelings as they arise. Do you feel sadness, grief, anger, anxiety, or a mix of all of the above? What is the feeling that you are running from or overcompensating for? Can you be with this feeling? Can you allow it—even welcome it?

The more comfortable we become with our emotions, the more actualized we become as human beings. This is true even for "non-emotional" types, such as Type Five and Six, who operate from the head center. But we don't have to do this deep, often painful work alone. As a coach, I help my clients identify and access their true selves and clear the self-limiting beliefs imprinted by their early experiences.

It's important for me to note here that blocks that are deeply rooted in trauma, abuse, or neglect may carry too much weight of suffering for you to access alone or even with a credentialed coach. If you feel like you cannot access or work with your feelings, or if you are experiencing anxiety, depression, or other challenges, please seek out a licensed therapist who can guide you through the emotional discovery and healing process.

Once I began to peel back the layers of my emotional numbness, I could feel a sense of lightness and ease coming through me, even as I sat with the sharp and fiery anger, pain, and sadness that my child self could not allow herself to process or even acknowledge.

***

Looking back at my early childhood, I could easily see how my natural personality patterns as an Achiever were triggered and exacerbated by my experiences with my mother and family. However, although the feeling of being in a vise grip eased a bit once I was old enough to go to college and make more

55

of my own choices, my pattern of overachieving didn't stop. In fact, it kicked into high gear after a life-changing trip to Ecuador and an encounter with new peers who could actually see my worth and potential.

QUESTIONS FOR REFLECTION

- Is there anything in your past that you are holding onto? Is this holding on keeping you stuck?

- What is one pattern from your past that you would like to start to release right now?

- Do you feel your emotions in the moment, or do you stuff them down or ignore them? Why do you think that is?

- Do any of your emotions scare you? How can you start to embrace the feelings you typically run from?

- What can you do on an ongoing basis to honor your emotions and allow yourself to feel all that wants to be felt?

CHAPTER
Four
4

BEYOND THE
BORDERS

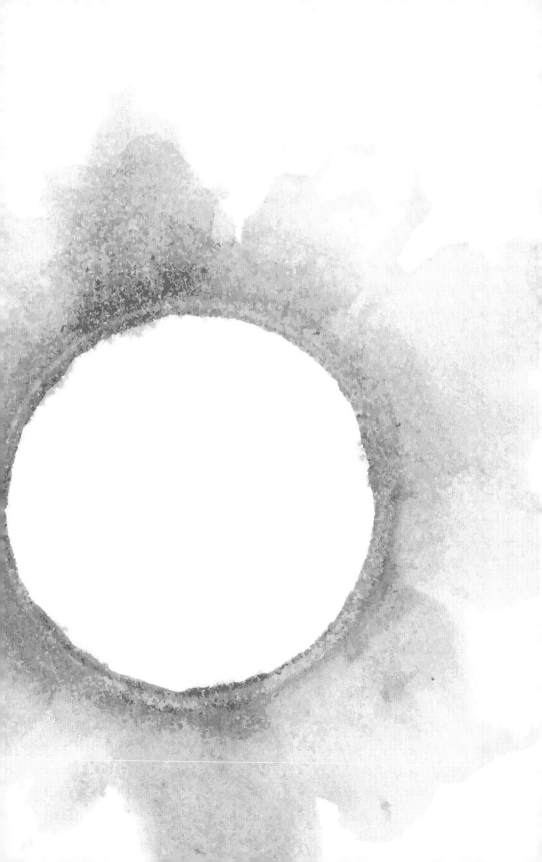

Beyond the Borders

After graduating high school in 1978, I enrolled in a two-year program to earn my dental hygiene license. In my second year, one of my professors initiated a public health mission to Ecuador in collaboration with the Archdiocese of Boston. I had been feeling drawn to the public health field during my dental hygiene training, and, of course I jumped at the chance to expand my worldview. Little did I know what a lasting impact this mission would have on my life.

Boarding the plane at Boston's Logan International Airport, I had no idea what to expect. I was still living with my parents in the public housing projects, and I was sure that I knew what deep poverty looked like; after all, I was living in it. In my teenage naiveté, I didn't know what to expect in Ecuador but I imagined I'd be walking into the Spanish-speaking version of Southie, with its run-down tenements and overcrowded apartments. I envisioned helping kids like me and families like mine.

When the plane landed, we were greeted by armed guards. This felt strange and a little scary to me. My curiosity only grew on the drive from the airport to Guayaquil, where we were staying. There were falling-down shacks and shanty towns everywhere. People were barefoot and dressed in rags. Parts of South Boston were pretty desperate, but I had never witnessed this degree of impoverishment.

Each member of our team stayed with a different Ecuadoran or expatriate family. I was fortunate to be placed with Nick Leondiris, the U.S. Consulate to Ecuador, his wife Ginny, and their son Jamie. I very quickly bonded with all three of them and felt more welcome in their home than I ever had with my family at home. There was a sense of warmth and acceptance there that I had never experienced before.

On our first day working in the *campos*, the rural communities, I was mesmerized by the beauty and innocence of the young children that we met. They were so excited to meet people from North America. They crowded around me, giggling, and looking deep into my eyes. I wasn't sure why they were staring at me more than my colleagues until I heard a young child say, *"Pelliroja!"* Then, I knew it was my red hair that intrigued them. Redheads are rare in Ecuador, and I certainly stood out. The children asked if we knew Michael Jackson, their pop idol. Surely, we must know him, since he was an American too? I hated to disappoint them.

As I spent more time with the children in the community, I could see that despite their deep financial poverty, they were happy. The kids found joy in simple games and daily activities, and their families were, for the most part, intact and loving. I recall being mesmerized by the love that was shared between the parents and children. I was intrigued by the loving way in which they spoke to each other and played together. This was so new to me, and my heart yearned for that kind of loving connection.

Most of the people we met lived in one-room homes on stilts with their entire extended families. Meals were prepared over kerosene burners, and everyone slept in the same open space. By the definitions I was accustomed to, these families should have been miserable—and yet, I had the feeling that they were worlds ahead of me in understanding what was really valuable in life.

The nuns, priests, and other members of the Catholic church in Ecuador impressed me in a different way. I was blown away by their commitment to their faith and their incredible devotion to the people they served. Among them, Father Frank Smith stands out most in my memory. Originally from London, he now lived and served in the largest slum in Ecuador, ironically called *Suburbio*. He trained as a nurse and had founded a clinic where he taught his community about good hygiene, healthy eating, and oral rehydration to save babies from dehydration (the leading cause of infant mortality in Ecuador and many other developing countries). Working with him was deeply inspiring, and to this day, I consider him to be one of the most important public health role models I've ever encountered.

Every day, the team from Boston and I worked with young children in Fr. Frank's community and elsewhere, teaching them about nutrition and hygiene, and handing out basic necessities. I loved watching their little eyes light up when they got their shiny new toothbrushes. What would life in America be like, I wondered, if every child felt so grateful for such simple things?

As we drove through the *campos* one day, our truck got stuck in a sand rut. Try as we might, we six young dental hygienists were unable to free the truck from the sand. Seeing

61

a tractor in the distance, we decided that half of us would stay with the truck and the others would walk toward the tractor, hoping to find a farmer. Soon, we saw several farmers over a hill in the distance. It was as if they appeared out of nowhere. They graciously freed us from the sand rut.

We had no money with us, so the only thing we could offer in appreciation for their help was toothbrushes. At first, they did not want to accept anything, but we insisted and gave them as many toothbrushes as we could. I'll never forget their kindness and their deep appreciation for those toothbrushes. That scene is etched in my memory and in my heart. It was a beautiful example of grace and gratitude.

The simple joys of life weren't the only thing I took away from my time in Ecuador. I also discovered a deep desire to end artificial inequity in both public health and other areas of life. I had always been uncomfortable when I witnessed prejudice and unfairness; I wondered, as a child, not only why some people got to be rich people (like the ones my mother said I belonged to) and others were poor and downtrodden like my family, but why people thought it was okay to treat each group so differently. Now, seeing the disturbing disparity between the wealthy class and the rest of Ecuador's population—a divide that made what I witnessed in America look mild by comparison—I discovered a deep calling to eliminate inequities and stand up for justice.

Before coming to Ecuador, I had decided that, after graduating from the dental hygiene program at school, I would attend a program for public health at Northwestern University in Chicago. After my experience serving the community in Guayaquil, I decided to change my plans. Setting my personal bar even higher, I decided, would allow me to serve in an even bigger way.

Some of the medical team, like myself, were there to work with children and families to improve public health and hygiene. Other members of the team, however, were surgeons and nurses who had volunteered their time to treat facial anomalies like cleft lip and cleft palate, and train Ecuadorian surgeons to do the same. After a long work day, the group would often come together for a meal and discussion. It was during one of these evenings that several members of the team broached the subject of dental school with me. If I were to become a dentist, they said, I would be able to have a greater impact in public health, even to the point of changing the system. They told me I was too smart not to pursue doctoral level training.

Needless to say, they were pretty convincing! The combination of my desire to make an impact in addressing inequities coupled with the unexpected support from the senior members of the medical team resulted in a seismic shift in my perspective on the world and my potential within it. At home, I was always defending myself and trying to prove my worth; here, people had noticed my skills without my saying a thing. It felt like I'd entered some sort of magical alternate reality.

I promised to give the matter careful consideration during my last few weeks in Ecuador. I'd be staying on with the Leondiris family after the rest of the team went back to Boston, and I was looking forward to having time to sort things out in my head.

63

I'd become even closer to the Leondiris family over the course of my stay, and was looking forward to spending more time with them outside of the demanding volunteer schedule. The daughter of a friend of theirs, Jennifer, would also be visiting from Maryland; we were the same age, and I looked forward to getting to know her better.

One day, all of us went to the U.S. Consulate to meet Nick for lunch. I remember smiling at the Marines who were guarding the offices, wondering what they thought of Ecuadorian culture and if they saw the local culture the same way I did. Later that evening, Ginny joked about how Jennifer and I were the talk of the consulate. "It's not every day they get to see American girls at work," she said. "They kept going on about how beautiful you are." I was shocked, but not just because the Marines had noticed me. That was the first time that anyone had ever called me beautiful.

Nick and Ginny also took us to visit various parts of Ecuador, and even on a deep-sea fishing adventure to catch a marlin. It turned out to be even more of an adventure than we expected. I mentioned to Nick that I was susceptible to seasickness, so he asked the consulate nurse for some Dramamine … only what he got wasn't Dramamine, but some kind of tranquilizer. I could barely stand up on the boat, and was so sick I thought I was going to die. Jamie was also ill, and the two of us throwing up in tandem only made things worse. Then, the guys actually caught a marlin as it was flying through the air. As they wrestled it onto the deck, it stabbed Nick in the leg. He was bleeding everywhere, which only made me throw up again. Finally, the skipper took pity on me and gave me a lime to suck on. As I made faces around the lime rind, he explained why British sailors were once called "Limeys."

The next day, I boarded a flight back to Boston with my stomach still in knots but my heart full of joy, contentment, and purpose.

Once I got home, the first thing I did was to drink a tall glass of cold milk. Neither the water nor the milk had been safe to drink in Ecuador, so we mostly drank bottled juice or soda. The second thing I did was take a long, hot shower. In my family's tiny apartment, with my siblings' voices echoing through the thin walls, I still felt like a queen in paradise. I couldn't believe how grateful I felt for something as seemingly simple as clean, hot water. It only reaffirmed my commitment to do something about the terrible conditions in which good people were living around the world.

A few days later, I formally canceled my acceptance to Northwestern University and enrolled in the pre-med/pre-dental program at Boston College. After earning my Bachelor of Science degree in 1983, I enrolled in dental school with the intention to dedicate my life to public health dentistry.

I returned to Ecuador to volunteer several more times throughout college and dental school. I also went to Peru and Bolivia. The cumulative impact of witnessing such poverty and seeing such suffering coupled with the commitment of so many wonderful people was truly life-changing. While for some, travel creates a temporary shift in perspective, for me these months abroad created a lasting change inside of me.

THE BLESSING AND CURSE OF OVERACHIEVING

I will forever be grateful for my time in South America. It cemented my desire to make a difference in the world, and showed me a path by which I could have a lasting impact. When I enrolled in dental school, I was young and naïve—but not as young or naïve as I had been. I had seen a piece of the world's injustice, and I was determined to right it.

What I didn't understand at the time was that my need to make a difference was a coin with two sides. On one side was the positive and genuine desire to serve others and right some very serious social wrongs. On the other was my constant subconscious need to prove my worth to those around me. The same inner drive that created a sense of determination and the drive to create change also reinforced my belief that I needed to work harder, do more, and be more.

That first trip to Ecuador kicked my overachieving personality into high gear. I embarked on a path of overachieving that didn't stop until my accident, twenty-five years later! I wanted more of the loving support and encouragement I'd received from the medical mission team and the Leondiris family, and I was passionate about making a difference for people who needed help. That combination drove me to push myself like I never had before.

This "personality overdrive" can and does happen to many of us. When the unconscious fear that runs our personality gets triggered, we react according to our ingrained patterning. When we aren't aware of this, and don't take steps to check it, we are off on a path of ego, and we abandon our true selves again and again. We become accustomed to our personality running our lives, and look in the same places for fulfillment over and over, even when we know that we won't find it there. As an Enneagram Type Three, when my personality goes into overdrive, the overachieving takes over. On my path to addressing inequities in health care, I obtained a Bachelor's degree, a master's degree, and two doctorates. I also completed two residencies. And as I became more and more immersed in my studies, I lost sight of what was in my heart, which was to help people. My overachieving shifted my focus from social justice toward career goals. I still brought my commitment to serve to my work, but my drive to gather more accolades was an unconscious parallel driving force.

Looking back, I can see that I needed to have that accident in 2005 in order to realize how hard my personality had been driving me. The problem with overachieving, as opposed to other personality issues, is that everyone thinks it's a good thing—even you! We are taught as children that, "If you only work hard enough, you can be, do, and have anything you want." In some ways, it's true—but to an unhealed Type Three, that's an invitation to become a runaway train. The positive feedback I received from others as I conquered one challenge after another only reinforced what was already a deeply-rooted unconscious pattern.

Now, I want to be clear: I'm not saying that I regret my educational path. I'm incredibly grateful for my education, my career, my colleagues, and my students, and for what I've accomplished. I know I've made a difference for thousands of

67

people around the world. What I want to bring to the forefront here, though, is that there is a fine line between healthy ambition and self-abandonment in the name of achievement. The key component in this distinction is motivation. Where is the desire to achieve coming from? Is it from a true desire to serve, or a driving need to serve the personality? In other words, my *heart* wanted to help people—but my *personality* told me that the only way to do it was to push myself to the limit. By the time I was woken up by that blow to the head, I was so numb and exhausted that I couldn't even *feel* my heart, let alone listen to its whispers. My personality—my ego, my false self—was running my life, and my heart was no longer getting a say.

When we are not present to our essential selves, it's easy for the ego to take over our life. I am aware now that when I'm running around without being present, ticking off lists of "shoulds," and doing instead of leading with my heart, my personality is running the show. When I notice this happening, I can create stillness and a safe "feeling space" to bring myself back to center.

Each of the Enneagram types has a particular way of "falling asleep" to the true self.

For *Type Ones*, a slip into perfectionism and the need to be "good" is an indicator that their personality is running the show.

For *Type Twos*, the relentless need to help others while sacrificing their own self care is a sign that it is time to wake up to their truth.

As I've described, for *Type Threes*, doing without being is the red flag that the personality is in high gear.

For *Type Fours*, a deep sense of not belonging and envy is their indicator that they are living from their false self.

For *Type Fives*, withdrawing from the world into the depths of their mind is their sign that they need to connect to their true self and bring their brilliance into the world.

For *Type Sixes,* the lack of trust in themselves, others, and the universe is a clear sign that the personality is running their lives.

For *Type Sevens*, their endless pursuit of excitement and freedom signal that they are living from their false self.

For *Type Eights,* their fear of losing control and not allowing any sense of vulnerability is a sign that they need to trust and open their heart to others.

For *Type Nines*, ignoring reality in order to keep the peace at all costs is a sure sign they are not living in reality and from their truth.

As we become aware of our personality type, we can also become aware of our particular pattern of falling asleep and letting our false self take charge of our life. It then becomes easier to step back into our essential nature and correct our trajectory so that it aligns with where we really desire to go, not just where we are being pulled.

If I had known as a teenager arriving in Ecuador what I know now, I might not have chosen the same path I did. I know that I would have been guided to service regardless, since a commitment to serve is deep in my soul, but perhaps I would have gone about it in a different, softer way. However, I see that every path I walked was part of my journey—and of the human journey of getting lost and then waking up to our truth.

QUESTIONS FOR REFLECTION

- Can you think of a pivotal moment or period of time in your life in which your personality went into overdrive? What happened?

- When did you notice that your life was being run by your personality/false self?

- What clues can you watch for to become aware that your personality is running your life?

- How is your life different when you are living from your false self versus living from your true self?

CHAPTER Five 5

THE DIAMOND HEART

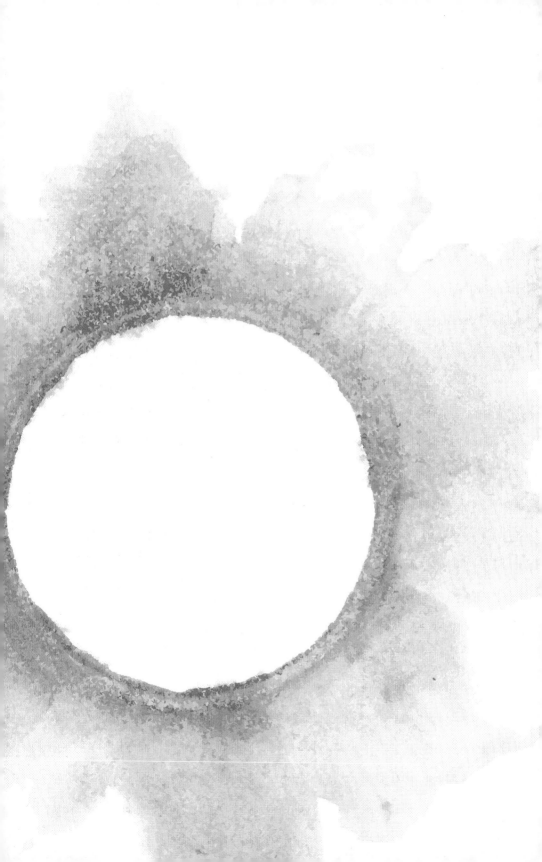

The Diamond Heart

"There's no going back once you start to wake up."

Don Riso's words have stayed with me since the moment he said them at an Enneagram training. I remembered them as I did the work of revisiting my past, uncovering the patterns of my ego personality that had shaped my life. And Don was right: now that I had started to do the work, there was no turning back. I promised myself that I would never stop searching my past and my present for the truth of my essential self, and that I would do whatever it took to live authentically, even when it was more comfortable to go back to my status quo.

I knew that, if I was going to continue to dive deeply into my life in search of answers, I would need support beyond what I could receive in intermittent workshops and trainings. I would need a community of like-minded people and an ongoing plan for personal growth. Russ and Don had often talked about their years with the Diamond Heart work; when I heard in late 2007 that a new group was opening in Boston, I knew that another serendipitous meeting of paths was before me. Of course, I signed up immediately.

As I read the work of The Diamond Heart's founder, A.H. Almaas, I understood why my heart had called me to this work. I found his writing to be incredibly clear, resonant, and profound, and it was as if he was speaking directly to my soul. When I read his work, I could literally feel the connection to truth in my body—the truth of existence, of reality, of being human, and the nuances of the soul's unfolding. I devoured and digested every word as if it were a bountiful meal.

I was particularly intrigued by the notion that I could be freed by living the truth of who I am—by living as my true self—and that this freedom is possible for all of us. But, I wondered, what did it mean to live as my true self? How could I uncover my true nature? I had already taken a deep dive into my personality through my work with the Enneagram, and now felt that I understood how I had come to be where I was, and why I had made the choices I'd made. I had a sense of who I was not—or, more accurately, who I no longer was, because I was choosing to move beyond the patterns of my personality— but now, I wanted to know who I was.

The Diamond Heart (or the Diamond Approach, as it is also known), is an evolving teaching which explores the many dimensions of human potential with the goal to create openness, freedom, and self-realization. It's not a religion, and doesn't rely on a guru to communicate its teachings. There's no dogma to accept. Rather, the work combines time-honored spiritual practices from various disciplines with modern psychology to help practitioners penetrate blocks and strip away the veils that hide our true nature.

My first Diamond Heart retreat was with about fifty other curious people, a few of whom I knew from my work with the Enneagram Institute. The teacher, who had a lovely sense of humor, explored with us the topic of presence, which at the time was still a bit of a mystery to me.

I recall an exercise in which we simply walked around the room and said hello to each other. We then paused, and did a short practice in which we sensed our legs, arms, and body as fully present in the room. We meditated from this place, and then repeated the "meet and greet." I was struck by the difference in our interactions before and after the meditation. Suddenly, I felt so much more connected to everyone. The people I spoke to seemed somehow sweeter, brighter, and more real. *What could have possibly changed in the last five minutes?* I wondered. Had *I* changed? Had they?

That experience has remained a touchstone for me. When I feel like I'm not connected to the people around me, when I feel isolated and closed off, I repeat that exercise and bring myself into a greater space of presence.

Presence is vital to staying grounded, being non-reactive, and truly experiencing each moment. When we are present, we are not living from our personality. We are not projecting our past experiences onto the person in front of us, or hedging against possible future events. There is something truly liberating about taking yourself off of autopilot and making choices from a place of truth in the moment.

In those early days of my Diamond Heart experience, I recall being deeply moved by the time I shared with the

75

other students. We were all so curious, just beginning to get a glimpse of the truth of who we were. We were like kids on a wild trek through the mountains; each new vista was a cause for celebration. I still wasn't quite sure how what we were doing would deepen my spiritual experience—many of the exercises seemed simple in the moment—but I soon saw that each time I met with the group, I gained some new insight, some new pathway for my thoughts and feelings. We were all just trying to make sense of life, and when we shared our "a-ha" moments in our group debriefs, we saw that even though our paths were not the same, we had more in common than we thought.

A year into the work, at one of our quarterly retreats, we did an exercise that showed us how much time, energy, effort, and resources we spent on our false selves—our personalities, the masks we wear for others—and how little we spend on our true selves. With two other attendees, I reflected on this inquiry. What I saw, and what I believe others saw, was that most of us do spend the majority of our time in support of our false selves. For example, I spent far less time in meditation and reflection, or walking in nature, than I did on my professional work such as research, writing papers, traveling to and speaking at conferences, etc. My life was crafted around the support of my false self. It wasn't that what I was doing wasn't valuable, or that I needed to isolate myself like a monk in order to serve my true self. But as long as my work was feeding my false self, and not my true nature, any time I dedicated to it would be in service of my false self.

I was blown away. I realized that I spent close to *90 percent* of my energy and resources on my false self—but that false self was not what would make me happy and fulfilled! How had I been blown so far off course?

I wasn't alone. All of us were experiencing this epiphany. It was at that moment that I knew without a doubt that I had chosen the right path with the Diamond Heart. I was learning things about myself that I would never have known without this experience. The freedom of living from our truth while experiencing the truth of existence was so enthralling.

After that revelation, we did a lot of work around our essential qualities—aspects of our true essence such as courage, strength, joy, power, will, and so on. (I shared some basics about the essential qualities and how they manifest for each Enneagram type in Chapter Three.) These are traits to which we all have access, but often they are mimicked by the personality in a false way. There is such a thing as false will, false strength, false joy. I began to be able to see the differences between essential qualities and my personality's attempts to replicate them. I also began to be able to see this mimicry more clearly in other people, and respond both with more compassion and greater awareness.

Our essential qualities are part of who we are. We don't need to strive to attain them, or work harder to make them more real. They are always there, because they are the core of who we are; all we need to do is relax into them.

When we don't allow this emergence (because of fear, doubt, or lack of trust) the personality tries to replicate this essential quality in a false, conditional way. For example, we all have access to the essential aspect of unity. But a Type Nine personality doesn't trust this, and so tries to create its own version of unity by maintaining peace and harmony at all costs. However, the personality can never recreate the essential quality in its pure state, so there is a perpetual sense of conflict, tension, and drama.

Our personalities also like to bury our essential aspects in order to validate their viewpoints. I felt for a long time that my life was so much harder than others' because my mother hated me. I was never held or nurtured as an infant or young child. And, in the Diamond Heart work, we spent a lot of time exploring the impact of our early childhood experiences on our present-day relationships with ourselves and others. But what was illuminating for me was not so much seeing the impact my childhood trauma had on my life—I'd already spent time exploring that in my work with the Enneagram—but learning that, despite my challenging early life, my essential aspects were as accessible to me as to anyone else. It was simply a question of identifying my self-images and allowing myself to experience myself on a deeper level. No matter where I came from or what happened to me, I was able to experience love, joy, and radiance. I was able to be strong, compassionate, and discerning. I was able to be my true self, no more or less than anyone else.

This realization gave me something I had never expected to receive: hope for a peaceful and fulfilling life. I knew I still had work to do (as we all do) to get there, but I could see it on the horizon now, like a beautiful garden waiting for me to step into it. And the best part was that this garden wasn't something outside of me, or a destination I had to push myself toward. It was me—my essential nature, in all its glory.

WE ARE BIGGER THAN OUR PERSONALITIES

The funny thing is, before my accident, I used to joke that I would have to get hit on the head to "wake up."

I think I knew, deep inside, that there was more to me than who I was being and expressing. I strove, I struggled, I achieved. I worked, and worked, and worked—and it was never ever enough. Consciously, I wasn't aware of how far I was from my true self, but there was a subconscious or unconscious knowing that came through in jokes like that one. Some part of me was asking for change—and the Universe took me literally!

I wonder, sometimes, whether I would have needed that whack on the head if I had been even a little more aware of and open to the fact that there was more to me than my personality. Hopefully, by reading this story, you won't need to be "woken up" in such a dramatic fashion!

Our essential nature can and does give us a depth of experience that the personality never can. As I practiced bringing myself into a place where I could access an essential aspect of my nature instead of the contrived personality aspect, I was struck by the quality of my experience. The sense of peace, well-being, and freedom was incredible. For example, the difference between relaxing into the essential aspect of strength and having to "be strong" was palpable on every level—physical, emotional, and spiritual. One was peaceful, flexible, and comforting; the other felt hard, sharp-edged, and exhausting.

So, why do we spend so much more of our time and effort on the false self? Because to be in essence we must be willing to see the whole truth of who we are—light and shadow, positive and negative.

As a person who values truth and authenticity, it was tremendously painful to me to see how much of my life had been lived from a place of inauthenticity. How had I spent so many years pursuing the exact opposite of my heart's desire? And how much time had I spent trying to be "strong," when all along I could simply relax into my essential aspect of strength? As I shared in Chapter Four, each Enneagram personality type has a unique way in which they "fall asleep" and let their personality take over; I was completely oblivious to the ways in which I was abandoning my heart in favor of achievements and recognition.

Seeing this imbalance between being in personality and being in essence brought me to one of my first dilemmas in the Diamond Heart work. If it was so easy and natural to embody our essential states, I wondered, why didn't we just live there all the time?

The answer came, in part, from our group sessions. When we began to explore our self-images and object relations—i.e., transposing our past experiences or relationships onto our current ones—I felt a whole new layer of unfolding happen within me. I began to see how many self-images I had, and how many the other people in my group were facing. We challenged each other to look at our self-images by providing feedback on what we saw in one another, and pointing out what felt real and what felt false. It was not always easy to hear this new perspective on who we felt we "needed" to be to survive in the world, but it was also freeing.

As you can probably guess, my self-images centered around being seen as successful, kind, good, and accommodating to the needs of others. As I explored why I held onto these images, I saw how deep their roots were, and how high their costs were for me. I wanted to be as kind, good, and likable as possible because I had grown up feeling wrong and shunned. I never wanted to be mean, or feel anger or hatred, because those would indicate that I was "giving in" to my family's ideas about me.

When we do not honor an aspect of ourselves, such as anger, we don't make it go away. Instead, it retreats into the background—but it's always running behind the scenes, influencing our decisions and fueling our false selves. If we don't look at the parts of us that we find unacceptable, we can never be whole. However, when we find the courage to look at those "shadow" aspects of ourselves—those painful parts we don't want anyone to see, or that we've pushed down—and bring them to light, we no longer need to spend energy feeding the false selves that protect those vulnerable parts of us. We can simply be more of who we are.

TWO INNER VOICES

Along with the aspects of ourselves which we suppress, the superego (aka, the inner critic) loves to build up our false selves. When my Diamond Heart teacher and I first started working with the superego, I was so relieved to learn that I wasn't the only one in the world who would beat myself up over every little transgression! This cruel, derogatory voice inside was part of the human condition. Who knew?

We would never talk with others the way we talk to ourselves. And just because our inner critic says something doesn't make it true! When we can differentiate the messages of the superego from our true knowing, we can disengage from them and instead look for our real inner wisdom. Doing this work has been immensely freeing for me, and has brought a greater sense of peace to my life.

Along with the Enneagram work, teaching clients to recognize and override the superego is a primary focus of my coaching work. When we can identify where and how our superego is running our lives, and learn to disengage from it, we can finally clear a path to inner peace.

Our superego can take on many forms. It can be quiet and insidious, or very obvious and loud. The important thing isn't how it shows up, but rather noticing how it takes over. For some people, there is a feeling of shame or inadequacy; others feel it as heaviness or contraction in their bodies. When we know the difference between our inner wisdom and our superego's negative messages, we can then make a choice about what is true and what is false. Instead of focusing on how we are "deficient" (because when we are living from the superego, we will always feel deficient in some way), we can turn our attention to our essential qualities of love, value, strength, etc., and ground ourselves in our bodies to come more fully into the present moment.

Our superego messages are often so ingrained in us that

we have difficulty distinguishing them. One way to begin to identify them is to remember that superego messages are always negative, and are often shaming and judgmental. Often, they are accompanied by a sense of heaviness, inertia, or internal shrinking. This makes sense when you consider that the superego is the part of us that holds us back from taking risks, going after our dreams, and believing in ourselves. It keeps us small. On the other hand, our intuition is a guiding force, directing us along our path of truth and wholeness. Your intuition is always positive, and will never shame you. Often, when you tune into your intuition, you will feel an inner lightness or brightening. Listening to and trusting this inner guidance is one of the greatest steps you can take toward freedom and wholeness.

The wonderful thing is, we can choose which to believe— the superego or our intuition.

Here's an example of how these might show up in your life.

When considering a new job that's a bit of a stretch for you, your superego might say, "Nobody will hire you. You don't have the skills to do that job. There are so many people who are smarter and more capable than you." This message might be accompanied by a feeling of hopelessness or futility. On the other hand, your intuition might say, "This position will allow you to expand your skills and explore new horizons. Plus, you might make some new friends!" This message might be accompanied by a feeling of lightness and anticipation.

In both cases, your situation, skills, and talents are exactly the same. The only thing that's different is which inner voice you choose to listen to.

I am continuously struck by how many people are living in alignment with their superego and not with their intuition. So many of us don't even know that the internal voice we're listening to is part of our false self and not our true nature. We simply accept its messages as truth, and live our lives accordingly. Until I began my own spiritual journey, I was doing the same.

The ego is designed to cover up the truth of who we really are. It feeds our false selves and personalities, and tries to mimic the essential qualities of our true nature, but it's impossible for the ego to get this right. This creates conflict and division. We go through our lives thinking our personality is who we truly are, and this leads us to create lives that fulfill our personalities but not our souls—just as I did for many years. We lose sight of the depths of our true nature.

One of the most powerful transitions I help my clients make is to become familiar with their intuition, recognize its voice and wisdom, and then act on its promptings. This involves identifying their particular superego messages and developing a practice of disengaging from those messages, as well as identifying self-images and object relations that get in the way of healthy and authentic expression and relationships.

We have so much in common on this human journey. The details may be different for all of us, but the challenges of self-acceptance, self-love, and uncovering our true nature are universal. There are many paths to enlightenment and realization, but all of them begin with self-awareness.

As my work with the Diamond Heart progressed, I put my new awareness to work. I began to explore even more deeply how I had let my false self and ego personality rule my life, not only as a child and teenager trying to prove myself to my mother, but as a young woman in her twenties and thirties rising through the ranks of academia.

QUESTIONS FOR REFLECTION

- What does it mean to be present? How do you know when you are present?

- What helps you to become more present?

- What habits/patterns do you notice in yourself? Do you think these are related to your true self, or to a false self?

- How do you respond when you hear the voice of your superego/inner critic?

CHAPTER
Six
6

THE
OVERACHIEVER

The Overachiever

*A*fter I got back from Ecuador, my overachieving shifted into high gear. Now, not only did I want to prove myself to my family and peers, I had a cause to uphold.

This new level of drive was underscored by the fact that school had always been a safe place for me. At home, I was either targeted or invisible. But, from elementary school (when I took home all the spelling bee prizes) to high school (where I was Class President and number two in my class), to college and dental school, I discovered that I was recognized, acknowledged, and respected in an academic setting. The difference between the two—home and school—was remarkable; unsurprisingly, school became my safe place.

When I landed back in Boston after my first trip to Ecuador, I enrolled in Boston College's pre-med/pre-dental program, with the intention to earn my Bachelor of Science in biology. It was too late for me to sign up as a full-time student for the fall semester, but it worked out, because I could go to school part-time and work part-time for that semester; since I was paying for my education, this was ideal.

I began as a full-time student at BC in January, 1981 and worked evenings and Saturdays. That summer, I worked as a dental hygienist in a local office, and saved every penny I could to pay for my classes. Father James Woods, then the Dean of the College of Advancing Studies at BC and now a dear friend, still recalls when I walked into his office to pay for my classes with cash. At the time, I had no idea that was unusual, but apparently the secretary was stunned.

As I plunged headlong along my new educational path, I began to forget the message I'd received as a child. I no longer trusted that everything was going to be okay. Instead, I felt very alone, like everything was up to me. Although I had great friends around me, I had no support from my family. I would always enjoy the moments I had with my grandmother, Catherine (Kitty) Hayes, my grandpa, John (as we called him), and my uncle Fr. Paul. I felt seen when I was with them; however, those moments felt too rare. As I got older, I fell asleep to my truth, and the trust that I had always carried in my heart. My personality was truly running my life.

Now, I've learned to recognize that when my personality is running my life, I feel a constant, underlying anxiety about having to do it all myself. Back then, though, it seemed like the aloneness was inescapable. If I could only do more, be more, achieve more, my ego said, I would finally feel okay again.

I worked very hard at Boston College, taking an extra class each semester since many of my credits from my Associates degree didn't transfer. Between my classes, studying, and my job, I worked myself to exhaustion. I actually passed out at work one evening while standing over a patient!

I'm not sure where I found the energy to continue, but I did. I earned my Bachelor's degree in 1983, and started my dental school training at Tufts University School of Dental Medicine later that summer.

I also got married during my senior year of college, when I was only twenty-two. Angel was my Teacher's Assistant in analytical chemistry, and a good, loving man.

I wanted to make it work with him, but we were on two very different paths. He had a close-knit family who wanted us to come to New Hampshire to visit every weekend, but I had to be in the dental lab working on patient cases, or studying for the next exam. It just wasn't possible for me to devote as much time to our relationship and his family as he needed.

I knew we were drifting apart, and he didn't want to go to counseling. Vacations together didn't do enough to bridge the gap. We separated, at my request, when I was in my junior year of dental school. When I told him I thought we should get divorced, he resisted, but later agreed. The last words he spoke to me were: "I understand, Catherine, and I'm a much better person for having known you."

The divorce was amicable, and since we didn't have any children or real assets it was pretty straightforward. After our court date in 1986, I never saw or heard from him again.

Honestly, the divorce barely scratched the surface for me emotionally. I was so ensconced in my ego fixation: my degrees, my achievements, and my accolades became my identity. As soon as the papers were signed, I dove right back into my work.

91

For many people, dental school would be the last step on their educational journey. They'd graduate, set up a practice, find some patients, and relax into the daily routine. Not me. My dental school degree was an interim step on my quest to create a career in public health, so there was still more schooling ahead. The end was not in sight.

I spent my childhood listening to my mother tell me how stupid and useless I was. Of course, these statements weren't aligned with reality; my conscious mind could clearly see that. But that didn't dial back my drive to learn more. My quest for knowledge was endless. It wasn't as if I thought about my mother's hurtful words as I pursued my degrees, but the message that she delivered was indelibly etched in my psyche. I was going to prove to everyone that I was not stupid, and my pursuit of this proof was as deep as the wounds she inflicted.

Just like my achievements were never enough for me, they were never enough for my mother. I graduated *magna cum laude* from dental school, and walked with honors. Later that day, my mother asked me, "Aren't you disappointed that you didn't graduate *summa cum laude*?"

I shouldn't have been surprised, considering that my mom could never give me an encouraging word, but her comment still stunned me. My dad, seeing my expression, stepped in.

"We're proud of you, Catherine," he said softly, patting my arm.

I smiled back at him, determined not to let my mother ruin my big day. "I'm proud of me, too, Dad."

I was proud of myself, but I didn't let the feeling linger. I was already looking ahead to my next challenge: a prestigious residency program at the Brigham and Women's hospital at Harvard University. A short few weeks after graduation, I walked through the doors at Harvard to start my new chapter.

LIVING IN REACTION

One of the things I learned along my journey (particularly through the Hoffman Process, which I'll share more about later in this book) is that we either take on our parents' patterns as our own, or we reject them. In either case, we expend endless energy creating a personality that is not in alignment with our true self. In fact, rejecting our parents' patterns uses up even more energy than embracing them, since we need to not only fight against our family patterning but also establish new patterning of our own. This is exhausting, and consumes energy that could be used for something much more productive, like following our inner guidance.

Many of my actions in my young adult life, I can now see, were about rejecting my mother's patterns. She told me I was stupid, so I made myself as smart as I could humanly be. She was cruel, so I made it my mission to be kind, and never tolerate meanness. She told me I wasn't worthy of living, so I created a life that others would see as worthy.

The negative messages we receive from our parents often become the narrative of our inner critic or superego. Abusive messages, in particular, can haunt us from within for years, even decades. These can motivate us to prove ourselves—or they can prompt us to act as though we are as despicable as our abusers said we were. Either way, whether we are rejecting or embracing, we become a self-fulfilling prophecy.

All of this integration, of course, happens on a subconscious level. We often aren't even aware that we are constantly reacting and responding to the voice of the superego. Our

93

patterns are literally running our lives. When this happens, we are no longer living our own lives: we are living according to someone else's rules.

I stayed in school full-time until I received my final degree at thirty-three years old. After that first residency, I took another residency, then got a Master's degree and a doctorate. I just kept going. Learning, achieving: these were my go-to actions. Schooling was, in a way, an addiction for me. Some people numb with drugs or alcohol, others with sex or gambling; I worked hard in school. I've often said, "Some people do drugs. I did school." It probably comes as no surprise that my first career was in academia. After all, school was my safe place; now, I never had to leave!

My friends and peers unknowingly reinforced this personality-driven path. After all, I was the living embodiment of success in academia; of course, to them, this was desirable and worthy of commendation. My multiple degrees, my awards, my academic career: these were looked upon favorably. What remained invisible was the cost I paid to achieve them. I was falling more and more deeply asleep to who I was, and nobody was noticing—not even me.

We all need an ego to survive. The ego is what keeps us safe. It keeps us from doing things that are genuinely unsafe, like pulling tigers' tails and jumping off cliffs. But when we live from a place of ego, and when we allow the superego to walk all over our hearts and intuition, we are not honoring all of ourselves.

Our personality is only part of who we are, not all of who we are. When we wake up to our unconscious personality patterns, we can honor the gifts of our personality while also recognizing that we are more than our ego. When I was pouring all of my energy into doing well in school, and after that, into succeeding in my professional life, I was not focused on cultivating what was in my heart. My desire to help people was being buried by my desire to prove myself to the world. If I had been as connected to my heart back then as I am now, I might have taken a different path in life, perhaps as a minister or theologian.

Don't get me wrong: I don't regret the path I took. I had a very successful career and I helped a lot of people. I worked with wonderful people. My public health colleagues are kind and dedicated professionals who are passionate about creating positive change in the world. But I'm also grateful that my accident began the process of me waking up to the truth of who I am: a heart-centered, compassionate healer and teacher. I have not thrown away my ability to get things done and be efficient, but those personality traits are now in service to what I am here to do, which is to help people move toward wholeness.

YOUR PERSONALITY SHOWS YOU WHERE YOU NEED TO HEAL

The amazing thing about the Enneagram and its personality typing system is that it not only shows you who you are, it shows you who you are not.

The personality patterns which belong to your Enneagram type are not reflective of the truth of who you are. As I've shared, my overachieving was compensation for my mother's rejection. It wasn't an essential quality of my true nature, but an attempt on the part of my ego to create the qualities of strength, belonging, and self-sufficiency that my personality felt I lacked. However, because the ego can never fully recreate the essential qualities of the divine self, I was trapped for years in a cycle of overachieving where nothing I achieved created the sense of fulfillment I sought. Only when I began to tap into my true essential qualities of strength, purpose, and belonging through the Enneagram and Diamond Heart work was I able to set my personality aside and ask myself, "Who am I, really? And what do I truly want?"

As it turns out, I'm not the hyper-driven achiever I thought I was. I thrive in stillness, where I can hear the voice of my heart and listen to its calling. I can support others in a group setting without always having to be the shining star. That low-level anxiety I mentioned earlier, which was once my everyday norm, is now my cue to slow down and tune in. My personality once pushed me to be someone I was not, to fall asleep to my own truth. Now, I keep a close eye on it, and take steps to reconnect with my true, essential self whenever my Type Three drive to achieve rears its head. It's not that achievement is wrong, it's just that, when I push myself to achieve for the wrong reasons, it undercuts my connection to my true self, my Source, and, most importantly, to my Basic Trust, that deep inner knowing that everything is going to be okay.

I've mentioned before that each Enneagram personality type

is unconsciously compensating for a feeling of disconnection from its divine, essential nature. The personality is created around a need to "make up for" some perceived lack of wholeness. But here's the thing: when the personality is dominant, we are no longer able to connect to Basic Trust, hear the voices of our heart and intuition, or access our path of growth.

Here's how this compensation looks for each Enneagram personality type:

Type Ones, when the personality is in control, are always trying to seek perfection in themselves and others. They cannot fully connect to Basic Trust, which tells them that they are already whole, perfect, and free. When the person becomes present to this underlying fear that they are somehow flawed, they can have more compassion for themselves, and take on the quality of freedom like a healthy Type Seven, their point of integration.

Type Twos' endless need to help and nurture others comes from their unconscious fear that they are unloved or unlovable. When they connect with Basic Trust, they are able to take on the higher qualities of the Type Four, address their own needs without endlessly supporting and caring for others, and develop a true sense of self and altruism.

Type Threes are always seeking external validation to make up for a perceived lack of inherent value. When Basic Trust is established, they can bring on the highest aspects of the Type Six to become more centered in themselves and put their skills to work in community.

For *Type Four* personalities, there is an underlying need to stand out and be "special" and unique in response to an underlying unconscious fear that they have no identity. As the personality begins to lessen its hold, they become more connected to a sense of purpose and mission like the Type One, their point of integration, and are better able to see what they have in common with fellow humans, instead of seeing the differences.

Type Fives whose personalities are running the show might feel like no amount of knowledge can make them competent, so they continually overthink every action and decision. Fives tend to hold themselves back from the world and in relationships when they are operating out of the unconscious fear that they are incapable. As they become more present to this fear, they bring on their true gift of clarity, and develop expertise in their chosen field, which in turn gives them confidence to step into the world as leaders like the Type Eight, their point of integration.

Type Six personalities are relentlessly trying to create a sense of security by mapping out plans and having things all figured out. They live in their heads, and are constantly playing the "what if" game and troubleshooting every situation. As they begin to release this unconscious fear and step into the trust that they are always divinely supported, they become serene, grounded, and truly peaceful, like a healthy Type Nine.

Type Sevens who are exhausting themselves by continually seeking new experiences will almost always struggle with anxiety, restlessness, and dissatisfaction. However, when the personality is recognized and allowed to let go of the reins, they are able to see that true freedom comes from being present and delving into their current experience, not just the ones to come. They take on the highest qualities of the Type Five, and no longer fear that they might be "missing out" on life, because the most exciting and interesting things are happening right here in the present moment.

For *Type Eights*, their behavior is a reaction to the underlying unconscious fear that they must remain in control. This leads to domination, and sometimes even bullying; these cover up a deep fear of vulnerability. As the personality loses its grip, vulnerability and openheartedness come forward, and they are able to bring on the beautiful nurturing qualities of the Type Two, and become genuinely compassionate.

Type Nines carry a deep fear that there is no unity or oneness; thus, their connections with others must be maintained at all costs. This leads them to deny their own will in order to keep the peace with others. As the personality lets go, they become self-accepting and self-inspiring like a healthy Type Three, and commit to pursuing their own dreams and life purpose in service to the whole.

***

If you are willing and able to see your personality as a tool for growth, rather than the sum total of who you are, you will learn to have compassion for yourself and begin to understand what's underneath your unconscious behavior patterns. As we develop this compassion and self-awareness we not only move up the levels of health and our own Enneagram type, releasing our personality and embracing our essential self, we also bring on the gifts of the point of integration for our type as described above. We can see how self-knowledge and self-compassion are tremendous and necessary catalysts for our move toward wholeness, and take steps to bring more of those qualities into our lives every single day.

QUESTIONS FOR REFLECTION

- What patterns from your childhood are you replicating or rejecting? What about your adult life is a reflection of or response to your childhood?

- How do you think these patterns have been running beneath the surface of your life?

- What do you think your personality and Enneagram type can teach you about how to let go of these patterns?

CHAPTER
Seven

THE HARVARD
YEARS

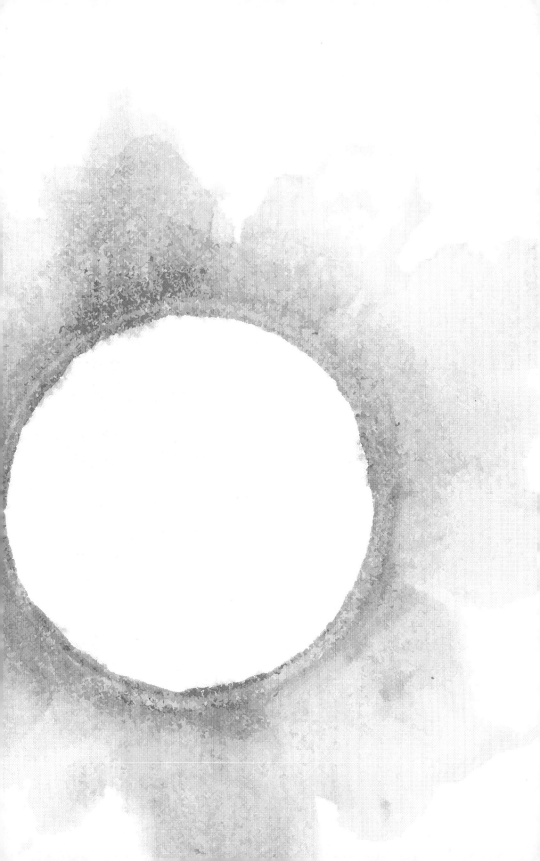

The Harvard Years

My residency at the Brigham and Women's Hospital was an exceptional educational experience. As a dentist, I treated severe dental emergencies and participated in the dental treatment of patients who were preparing for bone marrow transplants for cancer treatment as well as organ transplants. However, while the quality of the knowledge I was gaining was exceptional, it was difficult to see people suffering so much.

Upon completing my residency, I entered a combined program at the Harvard School of Dental Medicine and School of Public Health leading to a doctorate in epidemiology. Simultaneously, I also completed a dental public health residency. My whole life was devoted to reaching the next goal, the next certification. I was living wholly from my false self—and I had no idea it was happening.

Near the end of my residency at the Brigham, I got invited to a party. On the way over, I asked my friend who would be there. She rattled off a few people we knew, and then added, "Oh, and Vlad will be there too. Watch out for him. He's … difficult."

That should have been my first clue.

When we arrived, and Vlad and I were introduced, he was very charming. We flirted a bit, and he got my phone number from his friend who had co-hosted the party. Two days later, he called, and we started dating.

The relationship got serious quickly. Six months after that party, we moved in together, and a year later we were married. Fifteen months after that, our son was born—and the charming man who'd flirted with me at that party was nowhere to be seen. In his place was a monster.

Vlad was controlling and abusive. No matter what I did, it wasn't right. After we were married, he would berate and belittle me. When I got pregnant, he became physically abusive.

I didn't want another divorce. Honestly, I couldn't stand the thought that I might have chosen wrong, or that I had "failed." How could I have married someone who was so cruel? How could I not have seen what he was?

What I couldn't see clearly at the time was that I was replaying my relationship with my mother through my husband. Our childhood patterns are imprinted until we consciously release them; until we do, we will seek partners, friends, and other relationships that repeat behaviors and patterns that are familiar to us. This seeking is completely unconscious; it feels, to our conscious mind, like we get blindsided over and over. Only when we "wake up" can we consciously change our patterns to ones that support our personal growth, and move toward wholeness.

I insisted on marriage counseling, but nothing helped. It was clear that he could not take responsibility for his behavior, and in the end I had no choice but to leave with our son and seek help from my family. My parents were living with my sister at the time, and my sister invited me to come and stay there while I got back on my feet. I packed some things for me and my son and went to my sister's house.

So there I was, heading back to my abusive mother—only this time, I had a toddler in tow. I was in school full-time working on my second doctoral degree, and it was still not enough to please her. The lack of support I experienced in childhood was being played out again—only this time I was starting to get mad about it.

On the day my son was born, I looked into his eyes and marveled at the depth of love I felt for him. I wondered how anyone could hold a tiny miracle in their arms and feel anything but this overwhelming love and desire to protect. How could my mother have held *me* and not felt the same? What was *wrong* with her?

I held out hope that, even if my mother could never learn to love or accept me, at least she would love my son. That turned out not to be the case.

The first day that I arrived at my sister's house, my mother ignored me and did not speak to me at all that entire day. The next day, I foolishly asked her if she would watch my son one day a week while I was completing my epidemiology doctoral training at Harvard. Her response was, "Why should I help you? He should be *your* priority."

That was enough for me. For the first time in my life, I didn't shrink before her anger. I was thirty years old, a dentist and a mother. I wasn't a scared little girl anymore.

"He is my priority, and he will always be," I snapped. "And

how the hell can you talk to me about priorities? I was *never* your priority! You've been mean to me my whole life, and I will not take it anymore."

"Well, then," my mother sneered, "Get out."

Without another word, she proceeded to take everything that belonged to me and my son out of the cabinets. Bowls, cups, bottles, and clothing were all packed into boxes and set on the front steps. My sister and father were horrified, and asked my mother to stop, but she was on a rampage. My sister tried to get me to stay, but I could not and would not tolerate any more of my mother's abuse. I put the boxes in my car, scooped up my son, and left. After we were gone, my mother had my son's crib disassembled.

Suddenly, I was going through two divorces at once: one with my husband, and one with my family.

Somehow, we made it through. I was able to find an apartment, and keep our heads above water. Taking care of my son on my own wasn't easy, but I had no choice. After my mother's rampage, no one in my family would support me (except my sister Chris, who alone of my siblings wasn't afraid to buck my mother's rules), so child care was a real issue. What got me through was the memory of the day I decided to leave my husband.

Jogging around the reservoir near our condo one day when my son was about a year old, I was in turmoil. I knew I had to leave Vlad, but I was concerned about finances. I had a lot of student loans, and I was still in school full-time. How could I possibly support myself and my son financially? While I ran, I prayed for guidance. Suddenly, everything was crystal clear:

I needed to leave. More, I needed to trust that everything was going to be okay.

I could feel the connection to guidance; it was comforting and solid. My desperation eased, and I felt a sense of peace come over me, just as I had when I was six years old. No matter what—no matter how bad it got—everything really was going to be okay.

In the months after my divorce, I held on to that message for dear life. I had to trust, because if I didn't, I would fall apart. And, as I trusted, I started to take my first baby steps back to myself.

After finishing my doctoral degree in epidemiology, I took a faculty position at Tufts University. I had completed my dental education at Tufts and was excited to return to a traditional dental school to bring a public health focus. I was the only public health dentist at Tufts in my early career, and so had little mentoring in my career development. I stayed there for several years before returning to Harvard, where I worked as a full-time faculty member and a tenure-track Associate Professor until 2006, a year after my accident. I had many responsibilities: teaching, treating patients, administrative responsibilities, and my research. I was busy all the time, with little room in my day to simply *be*.

I also had no room in my life to feel gratitude for what I was accomplishing. That lack fed my overachieving, and also kept my shame running close under the surface.

When I observe myself—that is, when I look at my situation from the outside—I see a remarkably accomplished woman who, despite the odds against her, achieved so much in her profession. If I were an objective observer, I would be in awe of all that she did, despite the roadblocks. However, when I observe from the inside, I see that I never actually felt pride in what I accomplished professionally. It's an interesting dichotomy.

For example, when I received my Master's degree from Harvard, nobody from my family was interested in going to my graduation, not even my husband. So I sat it out. Most people (and most families) would be so proud at that moment, but for me, it was just another day.

In addition to all of my academic accomplishments, I was nominated for a MacArthur Fellowship (aka Genius Grant). I never allowed myself to feel pride in that nomination; after all, I did not receive the fellowship.

I was appointed by a federal judge in Massachusetts as an Independent Monitor to oversee modifications in the Massachusetts Medicaid program for a five-year period. My task would be to ensure that children covered under the Medicaid program had adequate access to dental care. It was a privilege to serve in that role, and I worked with many dedicated colleagues on both sides of the case, as well as a federal judge, the Honorable Rya Zobel. I recall when Judge Zobel told the Boston Globe that I was "very creative" and that "both parties have worked collaboratively to achieve these improvements and should be commended for their commitment to ensuring adequate access to dental services for the children in the MassHealth program."

While other souls would have crumbled, I soared, yet I never acknowledged that for myself. My unconscious shame always diminished my appreciation for myself and my accomplishments. So many of us go through this—and yet, somehow, despite our limiting self-images, there is a force inside of us that wants us to express all that we are. It will not be stopped by shame, or ego, or fear. It's more powerful than any identity or obstacle. This is the force which propels us to follow our dreams—the force which propelled me to write this book despite my trepidation.

Through the process of writing this book, I have had to accept and befriend both the shame of my past and a sense of gratitude for my achievements. This is what being human is like. This is what makes everything okay. All of our "broken parts" come along with us, but they don't weigh us down if we learn to love them.

***

My overachieving wasn't just reserved for my career. I was also an overachiever as a mother. I went on all of my son's field trips and to all of his games, and was occasionally the room parent at his school. I wanted to make his childhood as normal and loving as possible—as mine had never been.

No matter what my mother thought, my son *was* my priority, and would always be.

When he was around ten years old, I received an award from the Harvard Medical School Scholars in Medicine program. The families of all the recipients were invited, so I picked my son up from school and brought him with me to the university. It was the first time he had ever seen me get up in front of a group and talk about my work. On the way home, he turned to me and said, "You know, Mom, they gave you that award because you do a good job at school. But you also do a good job at home." Then, he put his arm around me. I will never forget that moment. It was one of the nicest things he has ever said to me. It made the burden of all the hard work and busyness fall away.

Every day, I got my son off to school in the morning before work, picked him up from the after-school program, made dinner, helped him with his homework, and put him to bed before diving into more of my own work in the evening. My goals, both for myself and for my son, kept me focused and moving forward—but I had so little time to appreciate the simple things.

To the outside world, I looked very successful and put-together. I had a good job, a steady income, and lots of accolades. But something was missing in my life. No matter how many goals I accomplished, it never felt like enough. I was so exhausted, but I just kept going. I didn't know what else to do. I had no idea how far away from my truth I had traveled, or how asleep I had fallen to my true self. My overachieving had truly taken over my life.

FEEDING THE SOUL

I was so accustomed to hard work that I did not realize that I had become like a robot, a machine. I had put so much on my plate that I had no time or energy to enjoy my success. It was hard for me to even take five minutes to savor the little things, like a sweet moment with my son. My mind was always focused on my future goals and the accolades and success they would bring. All of my concrete accomplishments were feeding my ego, but my soul was starving.

I had always been drawn to spiritual books. In particular, Louise Hay's *The Power is Within You* had a profound impact. I read it while I was in my thirties, and resonated with her story of overcoming hardship and trusting herself. At the time, I don't think I realized how impactful it was. I felt so hopeful after reading it, like there really was more out there for me— and then, I put it aside, and went on with my busy life. Still, something was opening in my consciousness.

Gary Zukav's *The Seat of the Soul* also really impacted me. I think it was comforting because it reminded me of the truth that I learned as a young child, which was to trust intuition and guidance. I also went to two weekend workshops on the Enneagram in the early 1990s and I remember being quite intrigued, but that sat on the back shelf for a while, too. Now, I can see that I was really drawn to a lot of spiritual teachings, but I was so overwhelmed by the challenges of being a single parent and so deeply sunk in the persona of the overachieving academic that I wasn't able to receive the wisdom that was right in front of me. I was touched by these books and workshops, and loved the understanding and sense of peace that came with them, but as soon as they were done I went right back to my busy life without really integrating any of it. Still, those moments of clarity were like seeds planted in my consciousness; when the time was right, I would reconnect with those truths.

We all have unique gifts that we bring to the world, and I believe that we are meant to share them in multiple ways.

Sometimes this requires hard work—but I don't think that the reason we are here in this human life is to just keep working ourselves until we drop. There is a richness and depth to life that we need to be still in order to experience. Our experiences and insights inform our worldview and perspectives, but if we want to integrate these with our true, essential qualities and use them in a way that transcends our personality, we need to be still enough to connect with our inner guidance, and open enough to learn to trust it.

I love finding ways to help people enrich their lives spiritually, and to go more deeply within themselves. I know from experience that life feels empty when we are simply working to keep a roof over our heads and going through the motions. When we get whispers, hints, and clues from the Universe, we should follow them; otherwise, those whispers will become shouts, and those hints will become, quite literally, whacks on the head, or other crises that we can't ignore.

During the period of my life when achievement and success were at the forefront, my false self was front and center as well, making all the decisions and processing all of the experiences and information that was coming at me. It's no wonder I wasn't able to process the spiritual information I learned! Every now and then, my true self would surface, but she would soon be forced back underground because the day-to-day activities related to my many responsibilities and my need for success overtook any desire or potential for a more spiritual journey.

112

Many successful people with whom I've met and spoken report stories similar to mine. There is a certain sense of emptiness in life when the focus is only on their achievements or being successful (in whatever form they've chosen). What happens when we reach the top of our field or the pinnacle of our career? What happens when all of our life goals have been met or exceeded, and there's no place left to go? What do we do then?

That emptiness is really a clue that the false self is in charge. Our true self, our essential self, doesn't present as empty. In fact, there is quite a sense of fullness, contentment, richness and peace that comes with our true self, no matter what activities we are pursuing in the world. We can touch into this when we meditate; the silence connects us with our true nature. We can also experience this when we spend time in nature, or pursuing creative activities like playing music or making art. Notice what connects you with this sense of peace and contentment, because you are inhabiting your true self in those moments!

The best way to differentiate whether we are living from our false self is the way it feels. When we feel frantic, unfulfilled, overly busy, discontent, or hopeless, our false self is at the center of our life. On the other hand, if we feel a sense of peace, contentment, aliveness, joy, and appreciation for the mystery of life, our true self is operating at the forefront.

When we are aligned with our true self, we can tap into and appreciate the guidance that is there for all of us. We listen to the whispers. We hear them. We follow them. We don't worry about having to figure everything out. We settle into the flow of life—and suddenly, life becomes so much more meaningful and peaceful. There is no sense of having to "go after" anything. There is a trust that life is unfolding as it should, that what is meant to be happening in our lives is happening and will happen. There is a letting go of the need to understand everything, a letting go of the need to have it all figured out, letting go of the need to have it all planned out. There is an acceptance of reality, whatever it may be in that moment in our lives.

Our suffering comes from fighting with reality. Instead of accepting what is happening and doing what is necessary to be with it and get through it, we wish it away. We long for things to be different, cast blame, get angry, or wallow in self-pity over the way things have turned out—but we cannot change reality. And so, we do one of two things: we fall into our personality to try to compensate for the reality we don't want, or we call on our true selves for guidance and the ability to see the lessons in the hardships. It's not our circumstance that governs how we feel and the choices we make; it is the perspective we take toward reality.

When we are aligned with our truth and with the truth of the universe, we are supported. When our personal will is aligned with universal will, we are supported. We are on a divine path and we will be supported as long as we keep that lifeline to our intuition and true self intact.

After my accident and the profound message that it was time to change my life, it was as if the Universe took charge of my life. Once I could no longer ignore my inner wisdom, I made some changes that I never would have anticipated. I also put things into place—such as those early Enneagram and Diamond Heart workshops—that acted as catalysts for life changes that I could never have figured out on my own. This doesn't mean that I was passive in my life—I didn't all of a sudden just start sitting around and waiting for things to happen—but that I participated fully in my life by tapping into my inner wisdom, the same wisdom to which we are all connected.

My accident was the universe's way of shifting me from a life led by my false self into a life led by my true self. The two are so very different. I'm not going to say it has been easy, because it hasn't. In general, our society values the life that the false self brings—especially when that false self drives us toward achievement, success, financial resources, and other "valuable" things. Our society doesn't value inner peace, contentment, fulfillment, and a mission-driven life in the same way—and yet, that is what I felt myself being called more and more strongly to live as I continued to examine my past and the "why" of my drive to succeed.

Before the accident, I used to joke that I was so stubborn that I would need to get hit over the head to wake up. I don't joke about that anymore. I *was* hit over the head, and I *did* wake up, and my life was never the same again. But even though I had broken free from the past that had bound me and the overcompensation that kept me too busy and distracted to fully live my life, there was one more major threshold I needed to cross before I could fully release my personality and the trauma that shaped it.

115

I had to forgive my mother.

QUESTIONS FOR REFLECTION

- How do you know when your false self has taken over your life? How do you feel when your personality is in the driver's seat?

- How would your daily life be different if you could completely trust that everything is going to be okay?

- How has the universe been whispering to you lately? What are the whispers trying to tell you?

- What decisions can you make today that will honor your true self and align you with your true nature?

CHAPTER Eight

BREAKING THE CHAINS

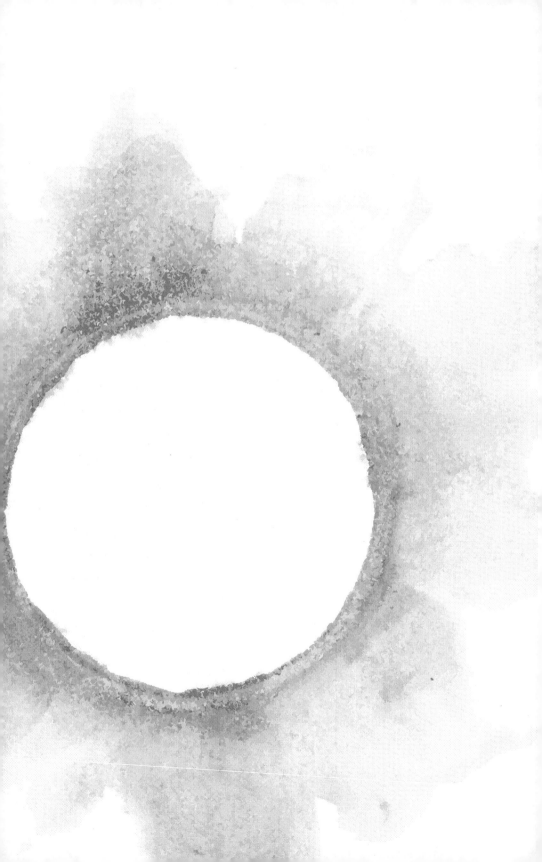

Breaking the Chains

A few months after my mom kicked me and my son out of my sister's house, I finally asked my mother the question that had been in my heart since I was a young girl.

"Mom, why do you hate me so much? What did I ever do to make you be so mean to me?"

My mother was sitting in her recliner in the living room. Since the moment I'd walked in, she had been staring at the ceiling. She hadn't looked at me once. Now, without so much as a hint of remorse or feeling, she replied, "Look, I gave birth to you. I did your laundry and I stayed up at night with you when you were sick. What the hell more do you want?"

"I don't know. Maybe for you to like me, or at least be proud of me? I'm a good daughter! I've never caused any trouble. I've always paid my own way. Would it really be so hard to say something nice every once in a while?"

Then, she did turn her head to look at me. The disgust on her face cut me like a knife. "Get out. Get out, and don't come back. I don't want to see you again."

With a heavy heart, I left. I didn't even say goodbye to my father, who'd been sitting quietly in his own chair through the whole exchange.

Within moments, I learned later, my mom was on the phone, telling everyone her version of the details of our encounter. God only knows what stories she made up. She was a master at crafting stories in which she was the victim—although, honestly, I don't know if she saw them as stories. I think part of her illness was that she actually believed her delusions, which may be why she was so easily able to convince others that they were true. At any rate, she informed those she spoke to that I was sick and evil, and that they needed to protect her from me.

Apparently, my dad hadn't been as unmoved by our encounter as he'd appeared. He gave my mom a stack of books on mothering, nurturing, and psychology, hoping she'd "see the error of her ways." My mom's response was to, quite literally, storm away in a fury. She was missing for days. (It turned out that she'd gone to the home of her childhood babysitter.)

Despite the fact that I was in the midst of a deep crisis of my own at the time, divorcing my abusive husband, and despite the fact that all I'd done was try to start a conversation, I was blamed for my mother's attention-seeking behavior. She was the victim, and I was the bad guy; it was the same old pattern I'd been contending with my whole life. I received hateful calls from family members, berating me for my cruelty to her. The distortion of reality across the board in my family was incredible. There was no curiosity about what had actually happened.

Between that incident and the dismantling of my son's crib after my mom kicked me out, I truly realized that I was never going to receive the love and support I craved from my mother, or from the majority of my family. I was truly on my own.

And yet, I still didn't hate my mother. I felt shame, sadness, and rejection, but I wasn't angry.

It was only after I uncovered my personality pattern through the Enneagram and went through the work of revisiting my past and calling in more of my true self that I realized I hadn't fully processed my pent-up emotions. The only way for me to truly put my past to rest was to forgive my mother—not just on the surface, but from deep in my heart. Only then could I rid myself of my patterns of overachievement and people pleasing and become a whole, happy, healthy person.

Not long after my initial Enneagram workshops, I was also guided to the Hoffman Institute and the Hoffman Process. Interestingly, Bob Hoffman created the Hoffman Process with Claudio Naranjo, a psychiatrist with expertise with the Enneagram. It seemed like an important synchronicity.

Through the Hoffman Process, I learned more about the self-limiting patterns I had taken on as a child and how they were holding me back from experiencing true love, wholeness, and fulfillment in my life. In order to excavate the anger, fear, and resentment that were buried under my mountain of shame and overachievement, I needed to go into a deep, dark place inside my heart that I had avoided for my whole life. Then, I needed to literally rise up through all the pain and anger until I got back to the light.

Getting in touch with my emotions—especially anger—on a visceral level became a vital part of my spiritual work over the next several years. The Hoffman Process was one of the first opportunities to begin the excavation of my heart; there were many more, some of which I've already shared in this book. That said, I would highly recommend the Hoffman Process to anyone. Most people have some things that we wish were different in our childhood; letting go of the sadness, regret, and resentment is a wonderful gift to give ourselves and our parents.

In 2011, my mother's health began to decline rapidly. By that point, I felt like I had come to terms with the way she'd treated me, and shed most of the iron cape of shame I'd been lugging around since my childhood. I'd unveiled my true nature through the Enneagram, the Hoffman Process, and the Diamond Approach. I'd cried more tears than I could count, and raged until I thought my soul would burn—and now, emptied, I was starting to fill up with better things, like lightness, love, and self-acceptance. But there was still a quiet corner of my heart that hung onto that anger, a piece of my younger self that screamed, over and over, "I didn't deserve this!"

When my son was about eight, we attended a family wedding together. There, he saw many of my family for the first time since he was an infant. In an odd and unusual gesture of kindness, my mother gave me the centerpiece flowers she had won. I accepted them, and she proceeded to invite me and my son to Thanksgiving dinner. It appeared that we were back in the family, at least marginally, but it wasn't long before we were shunned again. I was numb to it by that point, but it was terribly painful for my son, who had only just started to get to know his uncles.

My father's health started to decline sharply in 2003. I spent a lot of time in the hospital with him. As his final days approached, he often told me that he wished he could go to church one more time. "You've been to church every day for as long as I can remember, Dad." I reminded him. "I'm sure God will understand."

After he died, one of my brothers said to me wonderingly, "You were so good to him."

"He's my father, too, and I am a good person," I replied. I wondered if, for a brief moment, he may have actually allowed himself to see me.

I saw less and less of my mother and siblings after my dad passed away. By that time, I knew that I had a lot of work to do in the realm of forgiveness, but I also knew that my work was better done at a distance. While I know this isn't necessary or even healthy for everyone, it was important to me to put some distance between myself and my mother and siblings. I needed to protect my sensitive heart while I went through the process of accessing my feelings, and more wounds would only prompt me to close myself off again. I used meditations, visualizations, and prayer; in this way, I could "talk" to my mother with complete honesty, and experience a level of resolution that I could never have gotten from face-to-face conversations.

When it was clear that my mother was close to the end of her life, I knew that it would only hurt me and distress her and my siblings if I went to visit her. So, I worked with a shaman to send her love and peace, and to let her know energetically that I had forgiven her. In meditation, I visualized a conversation in which I shared with her all of my feelings about the years of mistreatment. I had the experience of her listening fully and apologizing completely. Then, she turned to walk away down a light-filled path. Mother Mary and Jesus appeared to guide her. For the first time in my life, I saw her face take on a look of complete peace. In that moment, the last pieces of hurt I had been holding onto let go, and I felt that both she and I were finally free. My mother passed away just hours later.

After a lifetime of feeling like I had to prove myself to a mother who could never be pleased, I was suddenly in a space where I could hold her with deep love and compassion. I saw her humanity, and how her own suffering led to her hurtful behavior. Somehow, I felt that we were destined to be mother and daughter; she was the catalyst for me to work through my life lessons. The pain of being so deeply hurt by the person who was supposed to be my biggest supporter and nurturer pushed me to learn things about myself and our nature as human beings that I might never have discovered otherwise. In the days after my mother left this earth, I had a constant vision of her being held in light, free from suffering and all of her human faults. I sensed she was hovering near so I would understand that she, like me, was more than her personality, and that she understood the pain she had caused as well as the depths of my forgiveness.

***

At her funeral, my brother gave a eulogy in which he spoke of the great value my mother placed on education. I did an internal eye roll, remembering how my mother had very nearly robbed my sister Christine of her opportunity to go to college.

Although I was the scapegoat of the family and bore the brunt of my mother's wrath, others were sometimes targets, too.

Chris, who is two years older than me, was the first of my siblings to go to college. My mother's cousins, Francis and Josephine, had saved a substantial amount of money and offered to pay for Chris's education—an incredibly generous offer. So, off Chris went to Fairfield University in Connecticut. During her first semester, she received a horrific letter from my mother, essentially telling her that she didn't deserve to be there, let alone have her tuition paid for.

When Chris came home for Thanksgiving, there was a lot of drama. I wasn't privy to what was happening at the time, as I was only sixteen, but I later learned that my mother had taken the money earmarked for Chris's tuition and spent it on herself. She couldn't stand to see her daughters doing "better" than her. Although it was never discussed, it's my understanding that she had to leave college to marry my dad.

Needless to say, my mom's cousins were furious, and took back their offer to pay both Chris's tuition and any future tuition for the rest of us. In one fell swoop, my mother had ruined it for everyone. Chris ended up staying at Fairfield by getting a work-study job and taking out loans, but I know she struggled. It certainly wasn't the supportive experience she had originally anticipated.

As my brother continued his passionate eulogy, I noticed that people were shooting horrified looks my way. I tuned back in to what was being said, and realized that, although I am the most highly educated of my family, my brother had completely neglected to mention me.

After the service, my Harvard mentor approached me. "Should I introduce your brother to you?" he asked.

Other friends and colleagues were similarly shocked at my brother's behavior, but I wasn't. It was completely in line with how my mother treated me, and how he was conditioned to treat me. Instead of being angry, however, I felt compassion. He was conditioned to see the world through my mother's eyes. He was never allowed to see me clearly when we were young, and it was obvious that he probably never would. Smiling through the glances and murmurs, I fully forgave him, too. I couldn't influence his belief—but I now had a much more clear and loving handle on my own.

THE REAL IMPACT OF FORGIVENESS

My spiritual path and my path to forgiveness were inextricably linked. Retracing my steps to my childhood trauma, then awakening to the truth of my feelings, allowed me to finally understand and be free of the shadow of my mother's illness.

Rather than just pursuing forgiveness in my mind, I had to feel and experience it in my body and heart. This was doubly true for me because Type Three personalities are heart-centered, but the same holds true for all personalities. Just because we understand and accept something in our conscious mind doesn't mean it's been excavated from the deeper layers of our consciousness, or from our bodies.

Pursuing the truth of my feelings and peeling away the anger and shame layer by layer allowed me to authentically forgive my mother and my family, instead of just thinking I had done so in my mind. Intuitively, even as I began my journey through the Enneagram and the Hoffman Process, I knew that forgiveness was one of the most important lessons I would learn in this lifetime. I knew I wanted to fully forgive my mother because forgiving her would set both of us free.

If we do not do the deep work of forgiveness, we can never be truly free. Our traumas, and the patterns they reinforce, will keep running in the background of our lives like broken records. We may not be conscious of the impact of our lack of forgiveness—in fact, our stories about why we can't forgive may be so ingrained in us that we become numb to them—but it is still there, keeping us stuck. With forgiveness comes freedom, peace, and an opening to love. We are more expansive and can allow the gifts of love, joy, freedom, etc. Without forgiveness, we remain closed off and apathetic.

For years before my injury and subsequent awakening, I worked to forgive my mother, but I see now that the work I was doing was not deep enough to be impactful—mostly because it was focused on my mother and what she did, rather than my own feelings about the events and how I internalized them. The first big shift toward real forgiveness happened during the Hoffman Process, where I found both a doorway into my anger and, simultaneously, a new level of compassion for my mother. The last piece, as I've shared, didn't release until after her death.

I want to be very clear about something here: Forgiveness does not mean accepting abuse, rationalizing mistreatment,

127

or returning to an unsafe situation. Forgiveness occurs in *our* hearts and *our* souls. It is an internal process, and sets us free. It is a gift that we give to ourselves—a pathway to our own liberation, not a free pass for those who have harmed us.

Forgiveness is also not about establishing better boundaries. Although boundaries are certainly important, and are essential to keeping us from experiencing more or greater hurt in the future, setting boundaries does not equal forgiveness. Forgiveness is liberating ourselves from our pain and patterns; it's something that happens inside of us, not something we need to enforce in the outside world.

The path to forgiveness isn't an easy one. It takes time, and it takes commitment. We need to be willing to be 100 percent honest with ourselves, not only about what has happened to us, but about our feelings around those events. It is not a one-size-fits-all process. Each of us has unique experiences, emotions, and memories that must be deeply explored and held with compassion before we can do the work of forgiving the other. We must know the impact our experiences have had on us, and not dismiss them. At the same time, we must remember that our experiences do not define who we are; we are not the sum total of our past. We are not aiming to create a sense of self-pity, or to wallow in our misery; rather, we are simply acknowledging the reality of our emotions and our experience, and cultivating compassion for ourselves, while at the same time realizing that life doesn't always have to be this way. We have the power to change our lives by looking at all the parts of our truth, and then working to heal what no longer serves us.

Because forgiveness is a process of "getting real," I couldn't access true forgiveness until I got real with my feelings. Clearly, others had figured this out before me (notably Bob Hoffman, who created large parts of his Process around forgiveness), but to me, at the time, this was a revelation. In order to forgive my mother, I had to stop rationalizing my mother's behavior, and my responses to it. Instead, I had to feel all of my fury at her.

THE SPIRITUAL VALUE OF ANGER

There's a common misperception in our culture that good people don't get angry.

Many of us want to be seen as "good" people—"spiritual" people who live a life in alignment with greater truths and a higher purpose. We don't want to feel anger, sadness, or other "negative" emotions because they aren't consistent with who we think we are, or who we want to become. But this eschewing of emotion doesn't work. We can't skip that step. None of us can.

I believed this untruth for a long time. I thought that if I just accepted the way things were and kept soldiering on with my life that I would eventually overcome my pain. What I didn't realize was that putting my feelings aside did not equal resolving them.

People who are spiritually evolved have a loving and honest relationship with *all* of their emotions—anger, shame, and sadness included. All emotions are normal, and human—and at some point in our lives we will have legitimate reason to feel all of them. It's not wrong to feel emotions. We simply have to

129

understand how to let them move through us and instruct us as to what needs to be healed, and how.

Some people have no challenges in accessing their anger, sadness, or fear. For them, the challenge is not to let these feelings rule their actions; instead, they must learn to let their emotions play themselves out before acting or responding. For me, it was the opposite. I had learned to treat anger as "wrong," because my young mind couldn't understand how to feel angry at my parents and sorry for them at the same time. It was safer and more acceptable to feel shame and guilt about my anger than to actually let it come through.

As I worked to understand and resolve this pattern of suppressing anger, I noticed that it didn't just rear its head inside my family dynamic. During a discussion with Andreas, one of my spiritual teachers in the Diamond Approach work, I shared the story of a particularly egregious policy violation by a colleague. As I discussed the situation, I realized that I actually felt sorry for my colleague, despite the fact that he had clearly done something very wrong. I was confused by this, and pretty frustrated. How could I be making excuses for this kind of behavior? What was wrong with this picture? When we dug a little more deeply, Andreas and I uncovered that this was an object relation. I was literally projecting my mother onto this interaction. Instead of feeling legitimately angry at my colleague, who had violated a trust, I felt sorry for him—just as I had always felt sorry for my parents. Once I saw the pattern emerge, I could finally feel the anger—both at the situation itself and at the pattern which had caused me to make excuses for my colleague.

After that, I began to see clearly how this suppression of anger was repeated, day after day, across my whole life. Through this awareness, I was able to start untangling my unconscious reactions and access my anger in the moment; when I did this, I could sit with it and let it pass without acting on or around it. One of the "safe" spaces to access anger for me was my car. When I was driving, I would keep the windows rolled up, so I could yell and swear in privacy, and not let any of the other drivers know how furious I was. My friends actually got a kick out of this, and would ask to drive with me so they could see "Mad Catherine" in action. It was like I had an alter ego behind the wheel!

I still have work to do around how I relate to my anger, but I have reached a point where I don't judge or dismiss it anymore. Instead, I sit with it. I feel the rage, and the sadness, and the guilt. I feel the grief, and let the tears come. I don't wallow in it, but I no longer dismiss it, either. I've learned that when we accept our anger as normal and human, allowing ourselves to feel it without shame or aversion, it doesn't need to run in the background, fueling our self-destructive patterns. "Realization" is the process of allowing ourselves to be *real*. That means feeling and working with *all* of our human emotions, not just the ones we like or consider "acceptable."

I also have learned that suppressing my anger prevents access to my essential qualities of strength and courage. As I've shared, when my personality is running the show, I default into overachieving and overdoing. When I'm doing these things, I can be strong and even courageous, but the ego's version of these qualities is always distorted and never as pure

131

as the essential version. By avoiding my anger, I was playing to the false strength of my personality. By embracing it, I can tap into my essential strength, which comes from who I am and not what I do in the world.

Each Enneagram type deals with anger differently. Several of the Enneagram types—like Type Three and Type Nine—have challenges in dealing with their anger, while other types process anger quite easily but struggle to work with other emotions.

The Type Eight personality has the least challenge in feeling and expressing anger. For the Type One, the anger can often be inner directed as they are hard on themselves for not being perfect. The Type Two, a positive outlook type, when frustrated with people not appreciating them, can feel and express their anger although not as directly as a Type Eight. The Type Four personality is comfortable with all emotions and feels frustration that other types do not dive as deeply into emotions as they do. In general, Type Fives do not easily connect to their emotions and often feel cut off from their heart. As they integrate to Type Eight, they are more able to access and express anger. For the Type Six, the primary emotion is anxiety or angst. Typically, their anger will show up as frustration. The Type Seven is a positive outlook type and depending on whether they have an Eight wing or not, they may not express anger easily and tend to look on the bright side.

In addition to knowing how our Enneagram type tends to process emotion, we can also access information about our emotions through our habits and the sensations we observe in our bodies.

On any given day, we experience a variety of emotions. Some, we can easily identify; others are so subtle that we barely notice them. We might not be consciously burying our anger or sadness, but we might observe that, when we're feeling "off," we automatically reach for comfort food, or a glass of wine. Both of these things distract us, and help us to keep our emotions under the surface. This "emotional bypass" is often done without any intent, and is very unconscious. As we begin to wake up to our emotions and notice their subtle shifts, we can begin to determine whether our daily habits are just habits, or if they are covering up something we were reluctant to feel and allow.

We are conditioned to believe that knowledge comes only through the mind, and that problems can only be solved on a mental level. However, our bodies hold tremendous wisdom. As I shared in Chapter One, we can access our body wisdom to connect more deeply with our essential qualities, which are always accessible to us when we stop overriding our truth with our ego personality.

Being true to yourself, accessing true forgiveness, and freeing yourself from the shackles of your past means allowing your emotions and feeling *everything* in a supportive, compassionate, self-loving way. To be truly whole means to know and experience all of ourselves, including the parts we have shunned, and completely forgive those who have done us wrong and contributed to the creation of our false selves.

Often, we need support to do this; the experience of asking for help, for some of us, can be a revelation in and of itself. My own coaches and spiritual teachers were instrumental along

133

my path to forgiveness. They provided support and direction at times when I felt lost and overwhelmed, and mirrored to me my own wisdom when I was ready to receive it fully.

***

Now that I have learned to access my emotions in a healthy way and have untangled so many of the detrimental patterns which unconsciously linked me to my mother for so long, I feel incredibly free. I feel immense gratitude for the anger, pain, and hurt I felt for so long, because these feelings led me to this place of greater peace and understanding. I also know that, when strong emotions arise, they are revealing something more that needs to be healed, and that, if I pay attention, the emotion will aid me in that healing. Each time I resolve a powerful or painful emotion, I know that I am becoming more of who I am meant to be in this lifetime.

All of my work with my emotions has had another, equally powerful effect on my life and perspective. After my mother's passing and my experience of total forgiveness, I began to question everything. I longed for an understanding of who I was without this pattern and the burdens it created. Who was I without my story of abuse and hurt? Who could I become now that I no longer had the daily burden of words like "You're no good," and "I wish you had never been born?" Who was I without my mother?

134

This quest for my true self became the focus of my inner work, and it led me to unravel the final pieces of my limiting patterns and beliefs.

QUESTIONS FOR REFLECTION

- Is there someone in your life that you need to forgive?

- What emotions are the most difficult for you to feel? Why do you think this is?

- Do you resonate with what you've learned about the way your Enneagram type processes emotions, particularly anger?

- How can you begin to excavate your emotions and experience all of your emotions fully? What support would make this process safe and accessible for you?

CHAPTER

Nine

9

COMING
FULL CIRCLE

Coming Full Circle

I firmly believe that when we commit to living in our truth, we are supported by the Universe.

I left my full-time faculty position at Harvard in 2006 because I was recruited to another university to an endowed tenured professorship and department chair position. For a variety of reasons, I left that position and began to develop my consulting business. Shortly thereafter, I pursued what was really in my heart, which is coaching and leadership training with a focus on cultivating greater compassion and awareness. I had experienced inspiring leadership in my time at the universities, and some leadership which was less so. I wanted to learn more about how to cultivate my own leadership effectiveness and coach leaders to be both inspiring and effective. (I always maintained, and continue to maintain, a faculty position at Harvard as a lecturer.)

The universe set forth a trajectory of change in my life beginning with the accident in February 2005. The deep spiritual journey that I embarked on one year later, through my work with the Enneagram Institute, continues today with my work with the Diamond Heart school and the work that I bring into the world.

Although, I look back with fondness on my first career as a public health dentist—and especially on my colleagues who selflessly contribute to improving the health of the public—the work that I do today is what I really believe is my life's work. I no longer separate my work from who I am, or feel like I have to ignore or abandon my heart in order to achieve greatness in the eyes of others.

My work now is heart-centered and aligned with my true self. Service and heart-centered leadership have always been a part of my life, however, that service and leadership now take the form of guiding others to live more peaceful and fulfilling lives by understanding, with compassion, their personality patterns and superego messages. It gives me a deep sense of joy and gratitude when I see my clients make lasting changes in their lives and their leadership approach. When they understand themselves more deeply and have compassion for themselves, their lives take on a whole new meaning, and the effects of living from their truth ripple out into their work, their relationships, and their communities. When I work with leaders in a corporate or non-profit setting, I help them lead from a place of authenticity, compassion, and Basic Trust, to the benefit of their entire organization.

I'm at a place professionally where it feels that my true self is at the forefront of what I do and how I live. This is a very peaceful way to live and to serve, and it's what can happen for all of us when we live this shift from our false selves to our true selves, and integrate this new way of thinking, seeing the world, and serving into our daily life. This is truly an authentic life, and I firmly believe that this is how I am here to serve.

Most profound of all the changes I've made in my life since my accident, however, is my shift back to the state of Basic Trust that I felt as a six-year-old child. Since I have made the shift away from my false self and into my true self, I now live in that state of peaceful trust every single day, and the message that "everything is going to be okay" is the guiding force of my life.

That's not to say that I don't still have moments of feeling challenged; I certainly do. In recent years, I've weathered the ongoing health crises of someone I love dearly, a house fire, and the death of a good friend, to name just a few. Each time I'm tempted to slip back into my old behavior patterns of overdoing in response to stress, I remind myself that, although every day is not going to be filled with bliss bunnies and rainbows, everything really is going to be okay. When I find myself feeling overwhelmed with the grief, sadness, or anxiety about what to do next, I remind myself that I am fully supported by the Universe. I find a quiet spot within me to reconnect to the silence and the trust that all will be well.

As human beings, much of our suffering comes from not accepting reality and trying to change the external circumstances of our lives before we've extracted their internal lessons. I spent much of my life and career doing precisely that: trying to change and outrun my childhood trauma. But, as I've discovered, running from or ignoring *what is* rarely results in anything productive. In fact, it often means running in exactly the opposite direction from what your true, essential self actually wants, which is wholeness, integration, forgiveness, and peace.

141

With my shift to a more spiritual life has come a much greater focus on what is happening internally. My reactions, my emotions, my desires, my hopes and dreams, and my connection to truth are so much more *real* than my prior life of high achieving. I'm not trying to say that we shouldn't strive for goals or set high standards. But if those outer trajectories are not balanced by inner wisdom, we will default to our habitual, ego-based patterns. When this happens, we cannot live authentically, or on purpose. We will be passengers on the runaway train of our false self.

All of the work that I've done on my own personal development allows me to integrate my deep belief in Basic Trust into my life, and to share it with others. I recognize that it took me many years to come to this place—but still, I'm often struck by the resistance that so many people have to this trust. Their ego personalities are still too much at the forefront for them to recognize that the perceived lack of wholeness for which they are compensating is just that: perceived. Not real.

Imagine a world where everyone, regardless of age, experience, or background, was able to trust that all will be well—a world in which we all could trust that we are supported in life, a world in which people live from the depth of their truth, and not from their patterns, their history, or their reactivity. If we all could see ourselves, and others, as who we really are, we would have both inner and outer peace. My mission is to bring that knowledge and ability to as many people as possible, in every walk of life.

142

THE WORK

Lasting change requires work, both inner and outer. Inner work, because we have to go inward to find the essence of our true selves and the wisdom of our hearts and intuition; and outer work, because once we know these things, we actually need to take action to change what needs to be changed and live differently than we have ever lived before.

In many spiritual traditions, the main description of the path is "the work." This is true for the Diamond Approach in particular. Looking at ourselves isn't easy, however it's essential to living an authentic life. To make lasting changes in our lives that impact our work, our relationships, and our inner peace requires us to look at our history, how it has shaped our patterns of behavior, and how it is still playing out in our current life. With compassion for ourselves and others and an openness to forgive ourselves and those who have hurt us, we have a recipe for enlightened growth.

There are a few things to remember as you set off on your own journey of growth and uncovering your true self. The first is that it's impossible, as a human being, not to have an ego/personality. Developing an ego is a necessary stage of human development. When we consciously direct our ego and keep it in its proper place, it actually helps us make our way through life. It is the lens through which we view the world, and part of what makes each of us unique. It is only when the ego or false self supersedes our true self and inner wisdom, and overrides our essential qualities, that it takes us away from wholeness. This balance is part of the human journey.

143

The second thing to remember is to feel and honor all of your emotions. However, you don't need to act them out or dwell in despair. Just because you feel sad doesn't mean your whole identity needs to be about sadness. Just because it is difficult for you to feel anger, as it was for me, doesn't mean that your whole identity needs to be built around rejecting your anger (or someone else's). A simple tool for reconnecting with trust and overcoming powerful emotions is to sit with your inner wisdom. Breathing deeply, feeling your body and the beating of your heart in the silence, you can allow your mind to clear so that your deeper truth can come through.

The third thing to remember is that it is vitally important to stay connected to your truth, no matter what stage of your personal journey you are currently navigating. If you follow your truth, you will always be guided toward growth and integration, no matter what your superego/inner critic has to say about it.

Something that has become very clear to me on my personal spiritual journey is that I have a profound love for the truth: the truth of existence, the truth of who I am, the truth of my interactions in relationships. As I remove the layers of ego that have obscured the truth in my work, my relationships, and inside me, I am more able to connect to who I am and what I truly want from my life. This journey to truth is the crux of spiritual practice for me.

My false self pushed me to achieve so that, on some level, I could prove to my mother and the world the truth of who I really was—a kind, intelligent, driven woman with a mission to serve. Now that I have peeled back those layers, truth has taken on a broader meaning and perspective. It's not just about me and who I am; it's about who we all are, and what we are here to do.

We are here to find and witness the truth of—the reality of—the beauty of this world, the beauty of human interactions, and the omnipresence of love. And the best indicator of our connection to all of these is our own human body.

I've discussed earlier in this book how our bodies can help us discern when our false selves are grappling for control. Recently, I've also learned that my body can be an indicator of truth. When truth is being spoken, or when I'm in the midst of a situation where a larger truth is present, I will feel a profound rush of chills in my body. It's a comforting and reassuring reminder that I can tap into truth at will, and this sensation has become a marker for me during my sessions with clients.

This truth-sensing skill has also been invaluable to me as I've made the transition from my academic career to my new career as a personal and leadership coach. As opportunities come my way, I now have a barometer by which to measure them. If they feel true in my body, I say yes to them, even if they feel uncomfortable or scary. If they don't feel true, I say no, even when they appear on the surface to be exciting or beneficial. If I choose to ignore this inner knowing, inevitably I end up stepping away from my true self and my true path of authenticity.

Each Enneagram personality type has its own relationship to the "virtues"—the essential qualities of the awakened heart which arise when we are living from our true self, not

145

our false self. The virtue of the Type Three is authenticity and truthfulness, so it's no wonder that I feel so at home and relaxed in the presence of my inner truth.

I'm at my best when I am fully expressing the truth of who I am and living an authentic life instead of in the contracted state of the ego that seeks validation externally. I trust that I am on the right path, even when I don't know where that path is going, because my truth is my guiding light.

TRUTH IN PRACTICE

One of the greatest gifts you can give yourself is to familiarize yourself with the way you feel and relate to truth in your body, mind, and heart. As I mentioned above, each Enneagram type has a specific "virtue" or expression of their unique truth.

For *Type Ones*, truth is in *serenity*. When they surrender to *what is,* they let go of the need to fix or perfect everything.

For *Type Twos*, *humility* is their greatest virtue. When they trust that they are loved and lovable, they become selfless and truly altruistic.

Type Threes connect to truthfulness through the virtue of *veracity*. Instead of focusing on external validation, they are inner directed and authentic.

For *Type Fours*, the virtue is *equanimity*. When they realize that they are more alike than different to others, they become self-aware and self-accepting and approach life with a more balanced emotional state rather than moodiness.

For *Type Fives*, the virtue is *non-attachment*. Their personality thrives on knowledge and forming opinions; when they embody this virtue, it allows them to let go of habitual ways of thinking and actually understand reality with a depth and perceptiveness that allows new and ever-deepening insights to emerge.

For *Type Sixes*, the virtue is *courage*. They truly feel the support around them and trust that they are guided. They trust themselves and others, thus letting go of the fear and angst of their personality.

For *Type Sevens*, the virtue is *sobriety*. When they connect to their truth, they no longer need to seek joy and excitement, instead they appreciate the simple and luscious pleasures right here, right now.

For *Type Eights*, the virtue is *innocence*. When they let go of their need to control, they no longer have to have such intensity. They become gentle and magnanimous, allowing instead of forcing.

For *Type Nines*, the virtue is *action*. When they no longer fear the lack of connection to others, they come alive to themselves and the world around them.

147

Based on what you believe to be your Enneagram type, how do you feel about your relationship to truth? Where in your life has truth found you through these pathways?

When we experience the virtue of our Enneagram type, we feel a sense of being called home, a sense of peace and belonging. When we relax our personality, it allows our essential qualities to emerge. Familiarizing ourselves with the wisdom of our body and heart is essential to knowing when we are living from our truth. Why? Because the body is more receptive to truth than the egoic mind is!

When you tune in to your body's wisdom (using the tools I shared in Chapter One), you'll start to notice your truth emerging. Often, wisdom comes through as a thought, a memory, guidance to a resource (like a book), or an indication to have a conversation with someone. The wisdom that comes through may not make sense to the mind, and that is okay. You may also notice that you are being guided toward truth through the virtue associated with your Enneagram type. For example, a Type Five might be guided to let go of an opinion in order to view a situation with less attachment, while a Type Nine might be prompted to take a particular action to become more alive and connected with their personal will.

However you decide to engage with truth in your life, trust it. Honor it. Follow its guidance, and be open to what transpires in your life. By doing this on a regular basis, you will begin to familiarize yourself with your inner wisdom and learn to recognize how it communicates with you. Soon, you will start to see the bigger picture, the touch of grace in everything.

QUESTIONS FOR REFLECTION

- Sit quietly and reflect on the virtue of your Enneagram type. What do you notice? What do you feel in your body? In your heart? What emotions do you feel?

- How does the virtue associated with your Enneagram type show up in your life?

- How can you bring more of your truth into your daily life? Your work? Your relationships?

- What is one change that you can make today to bring yourself into a greater alignment with your truth?

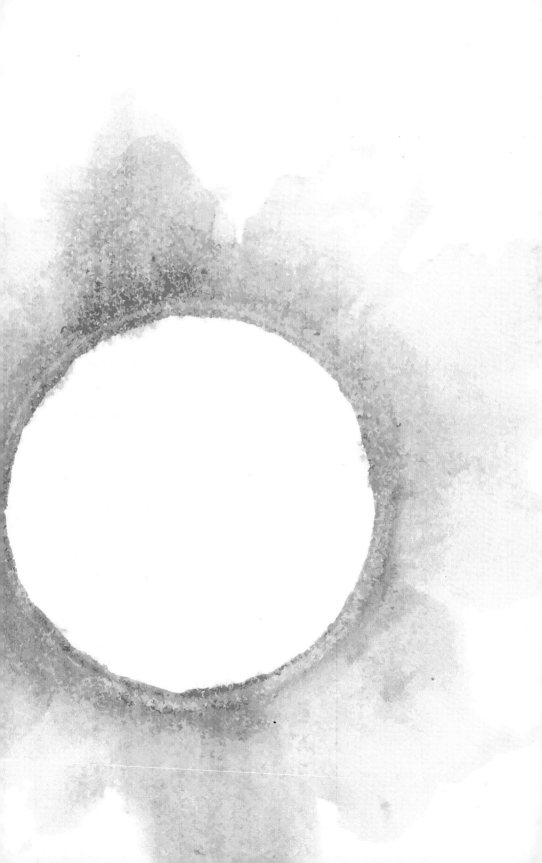

Afterword

Recently, I traveled to Egypt with a group of fellow spiritual seekers, including my teacher, Russ Hudson. While visiting the Cairo museum, I was drawn to a statue of a pharaoh. Others were already crowded around, examining what appeared to be a simple, if remarkably well-preserved, stone statue of a man in traditional garb.

I approached, curious, and Russ asked me to walk around to the back of the statue. When I did, I was overcome by tears of joy.

Gently perched on the back of the pharaoh's neck was Horus, the god of the sky, who protected the rulers of Egypt. His wings rested gently on the pharaoh's neck and upper back in a loving, protective embrace. I felt again the same profound and loving peace that I felt as a child on my way to school; a reminder of the deep, unbreakable connection to the divine that is ours as human beings. I felt blessed for having seen this remarkable piece of art.

There are so many instances in which I have been blessed by grace. My granddaughter, Camilla, is a perfect example. I never thought I would be a grandmother—and yet, here I am, grateful to be in the presence of a child who embodies so much joy, light, love, and pure spunk. As I write this, I await the birth of my second grandchild, who will be born right around the time the book is published.

We never know what life can hold for us. If we stay open to the blessings, I believe we will always be pleasantly, even miraculously, surprised. The accident that sparked this entire journey was a gift. In that moment, I was touched by grace.

I *am* touched by grace.

We *are* touched by grace.

You *are* touched by grace, even if you're having trouble seeing it right now.

It takes far more courage to commit to a full and peaceful life than it takes to commit to a life driven by our personality. It takes courage to look at ourselves, and ask the kinds of deep, sometimes painful questions that can inspire real change: "Who am I? What do I actually want out of life? What is the work I want to do in the world? What am I willing to do in order to step more fully into my truth?"

Being a coach is a privilege. I get to witness the unfolding of other human beings. As I listen to my clients, I listen with all of my being. I reflect back to them their own truth. I hear the things they may not even be aware they are saying. I remind them of their gifts, their strengths, their talents. I help them to see what makes them come alive, and what pushes them away from their essential self. It's exciting for me to see people embrace their truth—just as exciting as it was for me to embrace, integrate, and share my own.

As I step into this new chapter of my life—a chapter devoted to helping others recognize and live as their truest selves—the

152

message that I heard as a young child still resonates at my core. It carries me on the days when I feel less than strong. It reminds me of why I am doing what I do, and why it's important. And it shines through every time grace touches my life.

Writing this book is a vital piece of my spiritual journey because I truly believe that, during this lifetime, I am meant to help others to see how connected we all are to our truth and inner guidance. Although it may not always feel that way, and although it may not always be apparent, our inner wisdom is always operating, and prompting us toward our purpose and destiny. I have no doubt of this; my experiences tell me it is so. If I have emerged from the situation from which I came as a child—having two parents with psychiatric illnesses, living in the projects, and being the scapegoat in my family—and overcome all of that to connect with and live from my true, essential self, it is possible for anyone.

If that isn't grace, I don't know what is.

Everything is going to be okay—now, and always.

With love and great belief in you,

Dr. Catherine Hayes, CPCC

153

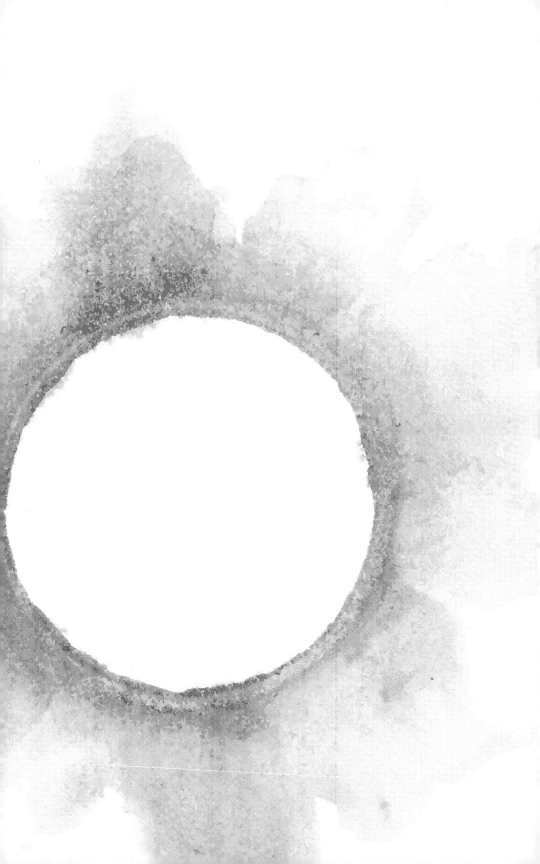

Resources

- *The Wisdom of the Enneagram.* Riso and Hudson. Bantam Books, 1999, ISBN: 0-533-37820-1

- *The Unfolding Now: Realizing Your True Nature through the Practice of Presence.* A.H. Almaas. Shambala, 2008. ISBN: 978-1-59030-559-1

- *Facets of Unity: The Enneagram of Holy Ideas.* A.H. Almaas. Diamond Books. ISBN- 0-936713-14-3

- Enneagram Institute Riso-Hudson Enneagram Type Indicator Assessment: www.Tests.EnneagramInstitute.com

- The Hoffman Institute: www.HoffmanInstitute.org

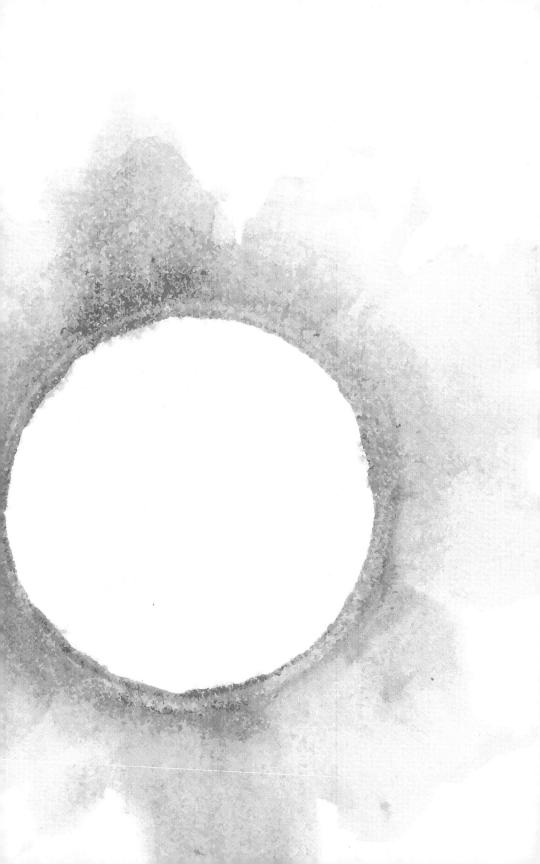

Acknowledgments

For years, I had considered writing this book, and knew it would come forth at the right time. I trusted that I would find the right team to work with me to make my dream a reality.

First and foremost I want to thank my gifted editor, Bryna Haynes, who encouraged me from the first time we discussed my book. Through her brilliance and her gifts, she assisted me in making my words and my story come alive. She is truly a gifted alchemist. I'm deeply grateful to her for sharing her gifts with me and walking with me every step of the way in creating this book.

I want to thank Linda Joy of Inspired Living Publishing for believing in this book and in me from our very first conversation. She has been so much more than a publisher. She is a coach, mentor, sage, and friend. I'm deeply grateful to her and her team at Inspired Living Publishing for helping me bring this book into the world: Rachel Dunham, Niki Gouveia, Nichol Skaggs, and Kim Turcotte.

I have been so blessed to have had and continue to have amazing spiritual teachers: Russ Hudson, Don Riso, Hameed Ali, Stan Grof, Leah Chyten, Peter Faust, Neil Carbon, Anne Laney, Gina Crago, Andreas Mouskos, Karen Dega, and the many other facilitators and teachers that I have encountered along my journey. I've been so guided and so blessed on this path of self-discovery.

I've had the privilege of working with gifted coaches who have inspired and supported me and my business: Hope Langner, Rick Tamlyn, Joan King, and Jeannie Spiro.

I want to thank Ann Casey, Deb Coman, Helen Santis, Leah Chyten and Kathy McGwire for reading earlier versions of this manuscript and providing their loving insights.

I'm appreciative of the clients who I have worked with over the years who have inspired me with their courage and commitment to themselves and to bring their best self forward. It has been and continues to be an honor and a privilege to work with you.

I also want to acknowledge my family: past and present, those who have left this earth and those still living, those who share my perspective and those who choose a different one. For my parents, siblings, and my son and his family ... you have all been a part of my journey and for that I am grateful.

I'm grateful to my beloved friends and my Diamond Heart community in Boston who have supported me over the years and through some very challenging times. They are too numerous to mention. You have touched my heart and graced my life. Thank you.

ABOUT
The Author

Dr. Catherine Hayes, CPCC

D r. Catherine Hayes, CPCC is a dual-Certified Professional Co-Active Coach and Enneagram facilitator with a DMD from Tufts University and Masters and Doctoral degrees in Epidemiology from Harvard University where she also completed a Dental Public Health Residency. She is a certified Executive coach with the Leadership Circle Profile™ and the Collective Leadership Survey™; an Authorized and Certified Riso-Hudson Enneagram Teacher and International Enneagram Association (IEA) Certified Professional and Accredited Teacher; a member of the Forbes Coaches Council; a speaker; and a highly-regarded influencer in the leadership field.

Passionate about bringing the true Enneagram into the world, she coaches leaders, individually and within organizations, to uncover the truth of who they are so they can live and lead from their highest potential. With the backdrop of the Enneagram and leadership coaching, she partners with clients to create transformation that brings more cohesiveness and productivity to the workplace.

Catherine lives with her family just outside of Boston, Massachusetts. Learn more about her leadership and Enneagram coaching, training, speaking, and workshop offerings at www.CatherineHayesCoaching.com.

159

ABOUT
The Publisher

Linda Joy

Founded in 2010 by Inspirational Catalyst, radio show host, and *Aspire Magazine* Publisher Linda Joy, Inspired Living Publishing (ILP) is an international best-selling inspirational boutique publishing company dedicated to spreading a message of love, positivity, feminine wisdom, and self-empowerment to women of all ages, backgrounds, and life paths. Linda's multimedia brands reach over 44,000 subscribers and a social media community of over 24,000 women.

Through our highly-successful anthology division, we have brought eight books and over 300 visionary female authors to best-seller status. Our powerful, high-visibility publishing, marketing, and list-building packages have brought these authors—all visionary entrepreneurs, coaches, therapists, and health practitioners—the positive, dynamic exposure they need to attract their ideal audience and thrive in their businesses.

Inspired Living Publishing also publishes single-author books by visionary female authors whose messages are aligned with Linda's philosophy of authenticity, empowerment, and personal transformation.

Recent best-selling releases include *Awakening to Life: Your Sacred Guide to Consciously Creating a Life of Purpose, Magic, and Miracles*; the award-winning *Being Love: How Loving Yourself Creates Ripples of Transformation in Your Relationships and the World*, by Dr. Debra L. Reble; and the multiple-award-winning *The Art of Inspiration: An Editor's Guide to Writing Powerful, Effective Inspirational & Personal Development Books*, by ILP Chief Editor Bryna Haynes.

ILP's family of authors reap the benefits of being a part of a sacred family of inspirational multimedia brands which deliver the best in transformational and empowering content across a wide range of platforms. Our hybrid publishing packages and *à la carte* marketing and media packages provide visionary female authors with access to our proven best-seller model and high-profile multimedia exposure across all of Linda's imprints (including *Aspire Magazine*, the "Inspired Conversations" radio show on OMTimes Radio, the Inspired Living Giveaway, Inspired Living Secrets, and exposure to Linda's loyal personal audience of over 44,000 women).

If you're ready to publish your transformational book or share your story in one of ours, we invite you to join us! To learn more about our publishing services, please visit us at www.InspiredLivingPublishing.com.

77906213R00106

Made in the USA
Middletown, DE
27 June 2018